Social work in the community

Making a difference

Barbra Teater and
Mark Baldwin

First published in Great Britain in 2012 by

The Policy Press
University of Bristol
Fourth Floor
Beacon House
Queen's Road
Bristol BS8 1QU
UK

t: +44 (0)117 331 4054
f: +44 (0)117 331 4093
tpp-info@bristol.ac.uk
www.policypress.co.uk

North American office:
The Policy Press
c/o The University of Chicago Press
1427 East 60th Street
Chicago, IL 60637, USA
t: +1 773 702 7700
f: +1 773 702 9756
sales@press.uchicago.edu
www.press.uchicago.edu

British Library Cataloguing in Publication Data
A catalogue record for this book is available from the British Library.

Library of Congress Cataloging-in-Publication Data
A catalog record for this book has been requested.

ISBN 978 1 84742 484 6 paperback
ISBN 978 1 84742 485 3 hardcover

Cover design by The Policy Press.
Front cover: image kindly supplied by John Birdsall.
Printed and bound in Great Britain by Hobbs, Southampton.
The Policy Press uses environmentally responsible print partners.

FSC
www.fsc.org
MIX
Paper from
responsible sources
FSC® C020438

Contents

List of tables, figures and exercise boxes

Tables

Figures

Exercise boxes

Practice example 1: Hasan

Hasan is a social worker working in a community mental health team. He is very aware of the government's new 'personalisation' and 'transformation' agendas that emphasise choice, control, prevention and the building of social capital (DH, 2007). He is, however, very sceptical of this agenda as all he deals with are emergencies. One afternoon, while visiting a GP practice, Hasan gets into a conversation with Anna, a health visitor whom he has met before. They discuss the fact that most of their work is on one or two housing estates mainly owned by a social housing association. They agree that the problems they encounter are similar and note that a number of professionals (social workers, health visitors, community psychiatric nurses, GPs, etc) visit in order to deal with the individuals who live there. Hasan and Anna remember the parts of their professional education that touched on community practice, and wonder whether there is anything they can learn from that to improve the lives of people that live on the estate, individually or collectively. What might they come up with?

Practice example 2: Irene

Irene is a social worker at a Sure Start children's centre situated in an ethnically diverse neighbourhood. Irene acknowledges that the purpose of the centre is to provide services to children and their families that are congruent with the needs of the community. Despite running nearly full workshops, parent and child activities, toddler playgroups and parent support groups, Irene quickly observes that the attendees are predominately white heterosexual women and white children. Considering her social work values and commitment to anti-oppressive and anti-discriminatory practice, Irene begins to strategise about how to make the centre's services more inclusive and appealing to those community members who are not attending, such as fathers, lesbian, gay, bi-sexual and transgendered (LGBT) parents or carers, and black and minority ethnic parents and children. Irene would like to see the centre as truly meeting the needs and wants of the community as a whole and not just a subgroup using and thus, further defining, the role of the centre. How can Irene meet this goal of including all community members in the programme planning and use of services at the centre?

Introduction

The above two practice examples describe two very different types of problems, but both will be familiar to social workers and to students on placement. The first practice example is likely to be the most familiar to social workers working in the statutory services, and could easily be transferred from this mental health setting to work with children and families, or to social work with adults. Many social workers in these settings find planning their work difficult when they are buffeted by the acute problems that hit them and their colleagues every morning when they get in to work. This first practice example highlights a common social work practice where social workers are faced with responding to 'emergency' or 'crisis' situations versus a practice that attempts to meet the needs of individuals in order to prevent emergencies or crises from happening. As is common in emergency or crisis situations, it may well have been that the service user Hasan went to visit at the GP office was already known to social services, but may not have been eligible to receive services due to falling below the Fair Access to Care Services (FACS) eligibility threshold. When service users fall below this threshold, often called non-FACS, they are not considered to be service users 'in most need', and therefore they and the community around them go on experiencing increasing difficulties until they reach a point such that their problems and difficulties are so severe the local authorities must accept the individuals as recipients of their service.

At this crisis point, with potentially all informal support having gone, the individual becomes a service user. The chances of them making use of the policy rhetoric of choice about services they receive and using them to regain control of their life is likely to be limited because of the crisis that has had to ensue before a 'service' is made available. A more restrictive outcome will mean a greater degree of marginalisation and discrimination experienced by this person. With the label firmly attached, there will be implications for all their relationships – with family, friends and neighbours, as well as with work colleagues and with their employer, if they are in employment.

This example goes to the heart of much that is problematic for social workers today, particularly those working in the statutory services. Many recognise that the most effective way of working with service users, both from the perspective of cash-strapped organisations and from the service user's desire to maintain control of his or her own life, is to prevent crises from happening where at all possible. Despite this, there are a number of factors that get in the way of this preventive approach to social work practice, and these can often include one or more of the following:

- The policy of 'targeting those in most need' first voiced in the community care changes of the 1980s (DH, 1989) has meant that resources are increasingly directed at people whose family and other informal resources are no longer able to sustain them in their independence in the community.
- The organisational practice of eligibility criteria (see DH, 2010) results in only those who are in substantial or critical need being considered for a service in most local authority areas (DH, 2002; Henwood and Hudson, 2008).
- The focus on the individual, with less regard to the community or network of support around them, reflects the ideology of health and social care which has, since the 'community care revolution' (Audit Commission, 1992) in the 1980s, focused on service users as consumers of care services in a spurious or 'quasi' (Le Grand and Bartlett, 1993) market. This ideology is also reflected in the way public concerns such as anti-social behaviour are blamed on individuals, with little attention paid to their environmental circumstances (Ferguson and Woodward, 2009).
- Social workers are less able to engage in constructive preventive work, or to look to informal networks of support within communities, due to their overwhelming workloads consisting of engaging with service users whose needs have reached high levels of crisis and dependency. High and intense workloads have been found to negatively affect staff morale (Jones, 2005; Unison, 2009).
- Health and social care services are experiencing an increase in resource constraints due to demographic changes, such as the increase in life expectancy (Means et al, 2008), and the national political and economic climate in which priorities for investment change and recession and bank bailouts have resulted in fewer resources being dispersed by government.
- Personalisation, focusing on the individual, can undermine collective services such as day care and residential care that were previously available (Ferguson, 2008; Ferguson and Woodward, 2009).
- Individuals continue to be marginalised, such as those with learning difficulties and mental ill health, due to medical model pathologising, discrimination and, worryingly, an increase in oppressive bullying within communities (BBC News, 2008). This marginalisation includes the continuation of paternalistic professional approaches in which service users are not informed of access to potential services or resources

(Baldwin, 2006) and a failure to see the collective needs of these marginalised service user communities.

The second practice example presents a very different set of issues and is one that will be more familiar to social workers or students working in the voluntary sector. This does not mean in any sense that the issues are not of relevance to social workers in the first setting, just that each worker is presented with a different set of priorities. Irene is dealing with people who have substantial problems in their lives, but she does not have to wait until an acute emergency arises before she is allowed to engage with them. She is providing a service to a geographical community and community of need, and her concerns are that she may not be reaching all of the people within that community, or addressing the needs that are most pressing.

While Irene may not have to deal with the pernicious effects of eligibility criteria in the way that Hasan has to, nevertheless, she will be operating a service that has become increasingly stretched, so some of the issues around resource constraints will be similar. It is certainly the case that the collective nature of the service provided will be under threat as organisations are increasingly focusing on dealing with the individual needs and risks posed by the friendless and unloved within some communities. In relation to this practice example, providing a more effective service to the whole community might be constrained by the continual marginalisation of people and lack of access to potential services or resources, through disinterest or lack of opportunity for professionals to look to informal networks of support within communities, or due to the continued failure of organisations and professionals to see the collective needs of community members.

The two practice examples highlight numerous barriers to a more effective preventive approach in social work, which are predicated on the notion that there are collective needs within communities, and communities are where most people wish to receive support while remaining in their homes and in their communities.

Exercise box 1.1: Incorporating 'community' into social work practice

In pairs or small groups, discuss the following:

1. In what ways do you think Hasan and Irene could take a community approach to their social work practice?
2. What would be the advantages and disadvantages to this type of approach?

This book is a resource in how to approach social work in the community. This introductory chapter provides an overview of social work in the community by defining the concept of 'community' and exploring why social workers should be concerned with this type of practice and what this approach might entail. Chapter Two then turns to an overview of the theories, values and critical concepts underpinning social work in the community, which provide the foundations needed to understand social work in the community; Chapter Three expands on this knowledge by exploring the historical and legal context of practising social work in the community. The book then turns to the specific approaches of community social work (Chapter Four), community development (Chapter Five) and community profiling (Chapter Six), and ends by looking at global perspectives (Chapter Seven) and the future direction of social work in the community, and how this approach can truly make a difference (Chapter Eight).

Concept of community

The concept of 'community' is often viewed positively, particularly when considering the strengths and resources that a community encompasses that can either help or support an individual, family or group in overcoming obstacles, meeting needs and promoting growth and positive change. Despite the numerous definitions of community found throughout the social sciences literature, with as many as 90 different definitions identified by Cohen in 1985 indicating the importance of attention paid to communities, there is great variation in its meaning (Cohen, 1985). The concept of community is often associated with a number of elements, such as geographical location, common characteristics or ties, social interactions, networks and relationships and shared sentiments (Hardcastle, 2011). One definition of community, proposed by Bellah et al (1985, p 333), encompasses many of these positive elements by indicating that a community is a 'group of people who are socially interdependent, who participate together in discussion and decision making, and who share certain practices that both define the community and are nurtured by it'. Based on this definition, community is more than a geographical place – it is a system that shapes people's thoughts and values, influences people's behaviours, provides resources and opportunities, and is a place where people live their lives (Hardcastle, 2011).

Despite this more positive approach to the meaning of community, most commentators have noted over the years that the concept of community is ambiguous, contested and often appropriated for political ends (Bell and Newby, 1971; Mayo, 1994; Gilchrist, 2004; Weil, 2005; Day, 2008; Stepney and Popple, 2008; Weil et al, 2010; Hardcastle, 2011). Understanding the concept of community is important, particularly due to the acknowledgement that how people respond to an idea will depend first on its definition and second on the power that the idea holds to create a reality for people. Therefore, we start from two general definitions of community because of the importance of their origins and relevance to social work in the community.

The first definition comes from the Seebohm Report (1968) that conceptualised and framed the new social services departments of the early 1970s in England and Wales. Seebohm (1968, para 476) stated that 'the notion of community implies the existence of a network of reciprocal relationships which among other things ensure mutual aid and give those who experience it a sense of well-being'. This definition has four key factors that we can see in other definitions. First, community is about *networks* that represent a set of interweaved relationships. Second, these networks are made up of relationships that have to be *reciprocal*, where each member of the network gets something positive out of the relationship. Third, communities ensure *mutual aid* where they are beneficial to the members of the community; and finally, the benefits of mutual aid are described as a 'sense of *well-being*'.

The second definition we explore here is that produced by the Barclay Committee that pondered the future of social work in the early 1980s and reported in 1982. The Committee's definition was of community as 'a network, or networks, of informal relationships between people connected with each other by kinship, common interests, geographical proximity, friendship, occupation, or the giving or receiving of services' (Barclay Committee, 1982, p 199). This definition expands on the one produced by Seebohm and is important because, even though community social work (Barclay's big idea) never really took off as a method of delivering services, it was (as described in Chapter Three) influential on the Griffiths Report (1988) which laid the foundations for community care. The Barclay definition notes again networks of relationships but adds some of the ways in which people are connected through these relationships, including by geographical proximity, common interest and the receiving of services, three areas that are commonly listed by other authors, in the definition of community by Bellah et al (1985) above (see, for example, Weil, 2005; Motes and Hess, 2007; Weil et al, 2010; Hardcastle, 2011).

There are several integral aspects to each of these definitions that are worth exploring in further detail, which consist of networks of relationships, a shared identity and creation of mutual aid or sense of well-being. We can see that networks of relationships are important and that these relationships could exist through a connection of people based on geographical location or based on a mutual interest such as culture, religion, health condition, sexuality, leisure pursuit or many other possibilities. These relationships are mostly defined as informal, where individuals have personal relationships with one another and an equal exchange of responsibility and obligation to one another rather than formal relationships, which are more impersonal and often based on a working and exchange relationship (Gamble and Weil, 2010). In this sense, the concept of 'community' can be seen as correlated with the concept of 'relationships', whereby individuals, families and groups interact with each other through a process of providing and receiving goods, services or support (that is, give and take). This process within communities commonly leads to an outcome of increased social capital which is defined by Putnam (2000, pp 664-5) as, 'the features of social life – networks, norms and trust – that enable participants to act together more effectively to pursue shared objectives'. A strong presence of social capital leads to an ability to form networks of trust and reciprocity within communities and has been found to be correlated with lower crime rates, better health among community members, lower rates of poverty, higher performing educational facilities and less anti-social behaviour (Putnam, 2000). Therefore, the strength of the relationships and interactions among community members may contribute to potential social difficulties or problems that often lead to interventions by social services. There is, of course, an argument that the predominantly middle-class areas have strong networks because they are actually more wealthy, healthy and better educated.

The network of relationships, or community, creates a sense of personal identity for each of the individual members (for example, young person or youth), but also a shared identity (for example, 'yoof' community). There is a debate about the degree to which a sense of community and shared identity is something owned and defined by the members of the community or whether this identity is imposed on them by the more dominant members of society (Mayo, 1994; Stepney and Popple, 2008). Social forces such as gender inequality, racism and class differentiation affect community relationships and identity as much as they do individual relationships and identity. For example, Mayo (1994) notes the importance of gender in structuring a very particular experience for women within the notion of care in the community where she describes the oppression and marginalisation that many women have felt in being seen or expected to fulfil the role of caring for people in their communities. The degree to which a community is believed to hold any identity has serious consequences for social work practice that wants to take that 'community' into consideration as a potential resource for the people living within it.

These oppressive social contexts are those in which communities are or are not expected to be self-generating or mutually supportive. Similarly, the social forces of racism still determine some welfare professionals' attitudes towards people from minority ethnic parts of the population. The last time one of our students heard the phrase 'they look after their own' from a placement colleague in response to a query about why there was so little take-up by black people in the locality was depressingly recent.

Part of the concern about the concept of community among authors is that politicians in particular use it as a purely positive or romantic notion that is hard to contradict as a source for good. Stepney and Popple (2008) discuss two approaches to community as a romantic ideal: first, looking back to past times when everything was more supportive, for instance, in an idealised village life, and second, looking forward to a time when we will be able to recapture that ideal if only we can put the correct policies into place. This latter notion is often used by politicians, notably by John Major (former Conservative Prime Minister), who stated that he yearned for the time when there were 'long shadows on county grounds, warm beer, invincible green suburbs, dog lovers and pools fillers and, as George Orwell said, old maids bicycling to Holy Communion through the morning mist' (1993). O'Hagan (2006) points out that Orwell also included 'queues outside the labour exchange' in his list describing Englishness, but Major chose to gloss over that!

We must consider the implications of these definitions and analyses of the concept of community. Based on some of the literature, it would be easy to dismiss the whole notion of community as either too diverse and complicated, too contested or too blatantly co-opted by politicians to have any worth for social work at all. Despite the presence of such literature, we refute this evaluation, and believe that people do have subjective belief that they belong to a community (Stepney and Popple, 2008), and this relationship, identity and network of mutual support is important to them. If people believe they are a part of a community, whether it is a positive or negative variable for them, then social workers need to take this into consideration given that the majority of their work is focused on individuals within those communities. If social workers want to make a difference in the lives of people they are working with, then they need to understand and engage with the factors that are important in their lives, and as communities represent one of these factors, then understanding the context of community is crucial. Therefore, social workers need to understand the communities that they work within and the meaning that communities have for service users, both to inform their practice with individuals but also to think about ways in which they can enhance the positive aspects of community for those vulnerable people with whom they work.

Exercise box 1.2: Defining 'community'

In pairs or small groups, discuss the following:

1. How would you define 'community'?
2. List the communities to which you belong/identify with, and discuss whether you view these as positive or negative, and why.

Social work in the community: why and how?

What is meant by the phrase 'social work in the community'? It is clearly a truism as all social work literally takes place in the community in its broadest sense, although we do have to be very careful about the way in which we define 'community' and 'social work in the community'. The majority of contemporary social work is tied up with an obsession on individualism, or what Dalley (1988, p 28) refers to as 'possessive individualism', which denies the context of community networks that support most people. This obsession with individual needs means that the external factors that construct the social conditions of people's lives – factors such as poverty, disability (using the social model), gender expectations, heterosexism, homophobia and racism – are often disregarded. Therefore, the problems people present to social workers are too often seen as purely belonging to the individual, it is his/her fault and it is, therefore, his/her responsibility.

A community orientation to social work redresses this imbalance and enables practitioners to see the broader social, economic and political factors that construct social problems. Rather than looking to purely adjust the behaviour of the problematic individual so that they fit the norms and expectations of powerful influences in broader society, a community approach avoids such labelling and stigmatisation (Becker, 1963; Goffman, 1963; Lemert, 1972), and enables the practitioner to understand the ways in which society is often pathological rather than the individuals who are so labelled (Leonard, 1975; Baldwin, 2011).

Social work in the community is congruent with the argument for the prevention of a crisis versus an intervention after a crisis. Most care and support for vulnerable people is located within the family, neighbourhood and community networks in which people live. It is a person's expressed choice (DH, 2006) as well as argued philosophically (Plant, 1974), from policy (DH, 2007) and practice considerations, that prevention is both effective and what people desire. Government policy has reflected the notion that prevention means supporting informal and semi-formal networks within the communities where service users live, rather than waiting until those are no longer viable and removing the individual to a much more costly service option. Therefore, it is necessary to see social work in this community context in order to enable social work practitioners and students to adopt practices which are more likely to 'make a difference' – a positive difference – in service users' lives. Social work in the community is important for a variety of reasons and, with additional planning, social workers can incorporate this approach into their normal social work duties. A rationale for considering 'communities' in social work practice is discussed below, with some examples of how social workers can incorporate this approach into their practice.

First, social work in the community is more effective than an individualistic social work approach because it focuses on sustaining supportive relationships rather than waiting for their demise. The approach favours prevention rather than crisis intervention, and building an understanding of the community, its needs, strengths and resources facilitates this preventive approach. Second, networking within the community builds an understanding of the resources, both formal and informal, available to professional staff and service users. Making links with voluntary and service user-led organisations is an effective way in to this sort of networking. A team could, for instance, invite key representatives of these organisations to discuss areas of mutual interest at a team meeting (Baldwin, 2011). Third, liaison, through information sharing and sharing of different perspectives, with other statutory organisations such as housing authorities (and housing associations), health organisations, schools and voluntary organisations, would enable practitioners to better understand a community by hearing different perspectives. It would also enable a community-minded practitioner to make their perspective clear to other professionals within multiprofessional and interagency contexts. Fourth, using available resources to carry out research and evaluation within the community builds an evidence base from which to make better judgements about the context for individual needs with which the team is working. Specifically, practitioners are in a good position to collect data about unmet need, and such data can provide a picture of the collective needs of the community they work within. Regular feedback of this data through the management hierarchy can result in priorities shifting to meet needs. For example, when one of the authors was carrying out research some years ago, he came across a team that noted the non-take-up of services by the older Somalian part of the local population. Collecting data and presenting it to management resulted in provision of additional resources to meet this need. Additionally, a student placement could be used to carry out a community profile, or another project such as developing a system for seeking feedback from service users about the service provided. Once this kind of information has been collected a team could use it to advocate on behalf of the local community for the collective needs of the local community. Fifth, a community perspective would encourage service users and the local community to be involved in decisions that affect them individually and collectively. There are systems within organisations to encourage involvement and partnership and practitioners should make the communities with which they work aware of these resources. Examples are consultation systems and complaints and representation systems. Signposting individuals towards collective organisations such as service user-led agencies could also enable them to have their voices heard through the relationship between that organisation and the local authority. Finally, the values of this approach emphasise the 'social' and 'collective' rather than the individual, so are supportive rather than isolating, and the values of social work in the community also reflect the social as opposed to the economic (Jordan, 2007). Therefore, the focus is more on making a difference in the lives of marginalised citizens rather than 'balancing the books'.

Social work in the community starts from an understanding about the ways in which broader social, economic and political factors construct the circumstances in which people then have to live their lives. Discrimination, oppression, poverty, social, political and economic exclusion are all aspects of these circumstances, therefore, which need to be understood and acknowledged when dealing with individuals, families groups or communities.

Summary and conclusion

In this chapter we have presented two case examples where social workers working either in the statutory or voluntary sectors can begin to view individuals within communities and focus on collective needs. We identified the common barriers to social workers taking a community focus, which often includes constraints imposed by agency policies, procedures and resources. Despite these constraints, we have identified ways in which social workers can begin to incorporate a community focus to their work in varying degrees. These include:

- thinking more preventively about social work practice versus reactive practice in emergencies or crisis situations;
- making links with community and voluntary organisations to expand one's knowledge about community resources and assets, as well as potential problems and difficulties;
- sharing information and work jointly with other statutory and voluntary agencies and organisations to better serve the individuals and communities who are accessing these services; and

■ considering the potential for community-based research to better inform social workers and agencies as to the needs, strengths and resources of the communities they serve.

This chapter also explored the concept of community and the ways in which communities are comprised of networks of supportive relationships, shared identities, and the creation of mutual aid or a sense of well-being. The creation of a community can be both empowering to those individuals who come together collectively to create an identity and supportive relationships, or oppressive whereby groups are predefined as a community based on a common characteristic, trait or geographic location that negatively separates the group from others. The ideal type of community will consist of networks that can provide potential mutual aid and improve the well-being of the citizens who live within them. Despite these variations in communities, we argue that social work needs to consider individuals within their communities, because individual and collective needs are both important and critical in providing social work services to alleviate problems, enhance personal and communal positive growth and development, and promote social justice.

Theories, values and critical concepts: the foundation of social work in the community

Introduction

Many of the theories and methods that social workers use in practice require or encourage the consideration of the community in various ways. For example, systems approaches require an assessment of the interactions and interconnections between a service user and her or his interpersonal relationships, community and environment (Pincus and Minahan, 1973, 1977). A strengths perspective requires an assessment of strengths and resources on individual, interpersonal, community and environmental levels (Saleebey, 2009). Empowerment approaches require an assessment of a service user's power and participation at the individual, interpersonal and societal levels with intervention strategies taking place in one or more of these systems to combat blocked resources and to enable service users to possess power and control in these areas that will contribute to positive growth and development (Greene et al, 2005). Finally, social constructionism holds that a service user's reality and way of viewing the world is not formed in isolation but is shaped and influenced by her or his culture and the society in which she or he lives (Greene and Lee, 2002). As illustrated, the concept of community and the consideration of its influence on service users is not an aspect that is ignored or taken lightly in social work, but rather is something that is interwoven into several aspects of the profession. This chapter provides an overview of the core theories, values and critical concepts that serve as the foundation to social work in the community. We start with an exploration of systems approaches followed by the theories and approaches of social constructionism, the strengths perspective and empowerment. We conclude with a discussion of the concept of need and an overview of anti-oppressive practice.

Systems approaches

Systems approaches are guided by systems theory, which is concerned with the interplay and interaction between systems, with a system constituting 'a complex of elements or components directly or indirectly related in a causal network, such that each component is related to at least some others in a more or less stable way within a particular period of time' (Buckley, 1967, p 41). Systems theory proposes that no one part, or element, of a system should be looked at in isolation, but rather must be looked at holistically by considering all elements that make up the system and the interaction and independence between them. In this sense, we see 'community' as a system made up of subsystems of individuals, families and groups, with all the systems taking on a role or participating in some way that creates the functional whole system (for example, community). Systems approaches hold the following basic premises as described by Teater (2010, pp 21-2), which are applied to a community as a system:

1. *The whole of the system is greater than the sum of its parts.* A community is viewed as a system with numerous elements or subsystems that interact together in order to make the functional whole.
2. *The parts of a system are interconnected and interdependent.* A change or movement in one of the community subsystems will cause a change of movement in other parts.
3. *A system is either directly or indirectly affected by other systems.* A community, as a system, can be affected by other systems, such as government, through policies or through society, by changing cultural norms or traditions.
4. *All systems have boundaries.* A community, as a system, has a boundary that makes it distinct from other systems, yet the boundary is permeable in that it is susceptible to change and influence from other systems.
5. *All systems need to maintain homeostasis or keep a steady state.* Communities need to have a balance within and among the systems where they can foster positive growth and development.

Systems approaches enable the social worker to step away from an individualistic approach to social work that is predominately guiding the practice that takes place within social work settings and challenges them to consider individuals within their environments and how the two interact, are dependent on one another and respond to changes that occur within the systems. Social systems theory is the crux of social work in the community as it acknowledges that the problems or difficulties that individuals may experience might not be best solved by intervening with the individual, but rather intervening within the environment or community to which the individual belongs. According to the social systems theory, fostering change within a community can, thus, create change among individuals.

Social constructionism

The theory of social constructionism is useful for understanding social work in the community and for explaining some of the key concepts associated with this approach to social work practice. The key text for this sociological theory is by Berger and Luckman (1966), where they explored the sociology of knowledge and examine how reality is created. Berger and Luckman were particularly interested in how man constructed meaning and created a reality that was individually specific, yet socially influenced. Reality is described as how people make sense of their world and the experiences around them. Berger and Luckman (1966, p 168) described the process of reality construction as follows:

> Man is biologically predestined to construct and to inhabit a world with others. This world becomes for him the dominant and definitive reality. Its limits are set by nature, but once constructed, this world acts back upon nature. In the dialectic between nature and the socially constructed world the human organism itself is transformed. In this same dialectic man produces reality and thereby produces himself.

The theory of social constructionism postulates that human beings are active participants in their creation of knowledge and reality, with the creation and meaning making being influenced by environment (such as family, community or society), where there are shared understandings, languages, values and norms (Berger and Luckman, 1966; Schwandt, 2000). The theory, therefore, values each person's life experiences and perspectives, acknowledging that individuals can experience the same event in different ways, particularly when influenced by social and/or cultural factors (Greene and Lee, 2000).

The four basic premises of social constructivism are very helpful in understanding individuals within their broader social circumstances:

1. Each individual has their own reality and their own way of viewing the world (Laird, 1993).
2. An individual's reality and knowledge is placed in an historical and cultural context with the reality they live their lives within developed through social interactions within these contexts (Gergen, 1985).

3. Language is used to express individual reality, again in social and cultural contexts, often through shared ways of seeing and modes of expression (Dean, 1993; Witkin, 1995).

4. There is no objective reality; there is no one truth (Franklin, 1995).

The social work task is always to make sense of the reality or the way of viewing the world that a service user expresses. If social workers try to impose their own views, believing them to be the only way of seeing the service user's world, then they are likely to misunderstand. Differences in reality may be based on age, class, sexuality, ethnicity, religion, disability or a whole host of other cultural and social factors that influence the way people make sense of their worlds. It is the task of social workers to understand, to interpret and to make sure that they have understood. England (1986) emphasises the importance of using our 'uncommonly common sense', in checking out our understanding with service users. Fook (2002) argues the use of critical reflection as we seek to avoid a practice based on assumption, prejudice or even oppressive belief systems.

The important point to raise here is the collective nature of these culturally and socially constructed ways of knowing. We are all individuals but we also often take on the values and attitudes that are part of our broader shared identity. A social worker who is not taking that collective perspective into account in making judgements about individuals or families is likely to make serious errors of assumption, prejudice and discrimination. If social workers are committed to social justice then they need to be able to see the connections between personal problems and broader social and political structures (Mills, 1959; Mendes, 2009). Failing to see these broader connections is a failure of commitment to social justice because it sees the problem as belonging to the individual rather than a societal responsibility, both in cause and effect.

Strengths perspective and empowerment approaches

The strengths perspective and empowerment approaches are critical to social work practice in the community as they both seek to assess the strengths and resources that are present within an individual, family and community system and to build on these strengths and resources in order to prevent problems or difficulties, creating an environment that fosters empowerment. According to Greene and Lee (2002, p 182), strength involves 'the capacity to cope with difficulties, to maintain functioning in the face of stress, to bounce back in the face of significant trauma, to use external challenges as a stimulus for growth, and to use social supports as a source of resilience'. The strengths perspective is relevant to social work in the community as it acknowledges that communities may be experiencing problems or difficulties, but within the community there are strengths, resources and abilities that are not being used, or are under-used or are currently being blocked from outside sources, which once uncovered, unblocked and acknowledged, can be used to combat problems and promote positive growth and development (Greene and Lee, 2002). There are six basic principles of the strengths perspective as described by Saleebey (2009, pp 15-19), which include the following:

1. *Every individual, group, family and community has strengths.* All communities are full of strengths and resources and have the wisdom and ability to transform and improve.
2. *Trauma and abuse, illness and struggle may be injurious but they may also be sources of challenge and opportunity.* Communities may experience traumatic events, but communities can also be resilient and can overcome adversity, growing stronger in the process.
3. *Assume that you do not know the upper limits of the capacity to grow and change, and take individual, group and community aspirations seriously.* We should not confer with stereotypes or labels placed on communities, but rather encourage the community to define themselves and to reach for their goals without restrictions.
4. *We best serve clients by collaborating with them.* All voices within the community should be sought, heard and valued, with the social worker working 'with' the community and not 'on' them.
5. *Every environment is full of resources.* Communities already possess strengths and resources, yet these may not always be recognised. Social workers should assess available strengths and resources to enable communities to fully participate in soliciting change.
6. *Caring, caretaking and context.* Human well-being is seen as related to caring. Relationships are often present within communities and communities should be encouraged to build on these relationships and to care for one another.

Based on these principles, the strengths perspective encourages social workers to identify, acknowledge and search for strengths and resources in order for the community to grow and to develop and use such strengths and resources to combat future problems and difficulties.

Similarly, empowerment approaches aim to challenge those systems that are preventing individuals, groups and/or communities from having the power and control over their lives or environments that enable them to meet their own needs and rights (Teater, 2010). Empowerment is defined as:

> The capacity of individuals, groups and/or communities to take control of their circumstances, exercise power and achieve their

own goals, and the process by which, individually and collectively, they are able to help themselves and others to maximise the quality of their lives. (Adams, 2008, p 17)

Empowerment approaches stem from the belief that oppression is a structurally based phenomenon that affects individuals and communities (Lee, 1996), and therefore requires social workers to tackle this oppression on individual, communal and societal levels. Empowerment approaches are congruent with systems approaches in that the focus should be on the individuals within their environments, thus the importance of seeing an individual within her/his community and a community within a societal structure and context. Therefore, social work in the community should aim to work with communities to create an empowering environment, which might involve challenging those systems that are preventing the community from having the power and control necessary to promote positive growth and development.

Concept of need

Social workers work with people who are, by definition, in need; it is therefore important to be precise about what is meant by the term if social workers are going to be clear about how they understand and meet service users' and community needs (Baldwin, 2000; McDonald, 2006; Sharkey, 2007). In order to steer our way through the complexity of this concept of need, ways of understanding it are needed – a theory or model of need that helps in both informing and evaluating professional practice. We begin by exploring three specific approaches to the concept of need: Maslow's (1970) hierarchy of need, Bradshaw's (1972) taxonomy of need and Doyal and Gough's (1991) theory of human need.

Maslow's hierarchy of need (Maslow, 1970) consists of the following five categories of need, which are built on one another: physiological, safety, love/belonging, esteem and self-actualisation. *Physiological needs*, such as food, water, sleep and sex, serve as the base of a hierarchy with a requirement that these needs be met for survival and in order to move up the hierarchy to the next set of needs. Above the physiological needs are further survival needs related to *safety*, such as security and protection. All human beings have a drive to meet these basic survival needs (physiological and safety), but Maslow goes further in theorising that human beings are also motivated by social needs – the requirement for a *sense of belonging and to be loved* – which is the next step on the hierarchy. Above the love/belonging needs are *esteem needs, or the need to be recognised,* to be given status in society and the need for self-esteem. Finally, at the top of the hierarchy, is the need for *self-actualisation,* or the achievement of a fully integrated identity that individuals can feel confident within as they live their lives.

Maslow's hierarchy serves as a useful theory for understanding the importance of meeting basic needs, such as physiological and safety needs, in order for there to be an opportunity for an individual to establish a sense of loving, belonging, self-esteem and self-actualisation. The theory may be useful in assessing whether an individual could grow, thrive and survive within a community by assessing the extent to which their basic needs are being met within that community and, based on the assessment, determining the type of intervention that would be most appropriate. For example, social workers cannot expect individuals within a community to become socially active or develop a sense of social cohesiveness if their basic physiological needs are not being met. Therefore, an intervention would involve meeting basic needs first before moving to interventions that encourage social cohesiveness.

While Marslow's hierarchy of need is a useful theory for understanding the ways in which human beings are always striving for more in pursuing needs, it is a very individualistic model based on individualistic societies versus a collectivistic society. In this sense, the theory is criticised as being ethnocentric (Hofstede, 1980, 1984), and has been found to have cultural limitations (see Haire et al, 1966) that do not take into account different interpretations of need. Additionally, Maslow developed the theory through his research on prominent figures within society, such as Albert Einstein and Frederick Douglass, and healthy university students, which leaves the theory often criticised as merely reflecting Maslow's US middle-class values (Hofstede, 1980). Maslow (1954, p 236) refused to include a diverse group within his research, stating, 'the study of crippled, stunted, immature, and unhealthy specimens can yield only a cripple psychology and a cripple philosophy'. Based on such critiques of Maslow's hierarchy of need, specifically its ethnocentrism and lack of consideration of different interpretations of need, an additional theory or model is needed in order to more clearly understand this concept.

Bradshaw's (1972) taxonomy of need is helpful in seeing different interpretations or perspectives on need. This model argues that there are four overlapping ways of understanding need in social policy, which include normative, felt, expressed and comparative need. *Normative* need includes those needs that are considered the norm and are identified by a set standard, for example, means testing in deciding who is in need of benefits. These needs are established and determined by those in authority positions who decide which needs to consider as important, and can therefore often be based on political, managerial or professional assumptions about need rather than the actual or felt needs of the local population. *Felt* need considers the subjective perspective of the individuals based on what people feel that they need. This type of need could be based on desirable rather than objective needs, which can be identified and measured. *Expressed* need is what people say that they need, which could be different to what they are actually feeling they need. It is certainly the case that sometimes people will not express the needs they feel they have for a number of reasons, including poor self-esteem and a lack of assertiveness, a belief that their needs are less important than others or because they fear the consequences of revealing a need that they feel might be perceived as a weakness. For example, an older person might underplay her needs to an assessing social worker because she may well be trying to avoid an outcome she fears, such as residential care. Lastly, *comparative* need compares needs that emerge among one group with a like group that does not present with those needs. Bradshaw's model suggests that needs are relative and not universal, which is a current argument to supporting the personalisation agenda that focuses on individual versus collective needs (see Chapter Three). The argument here is that needs are not static and/or easily identifiable as need depends on social, economic and political circumstances. For example, the needs of children in Darfur will not be the same as children living in Bath, England.

Finally, Doyal and Gough (1991) disagree with Bradshaw's relativist position, as they argue that there are universal needs that are for physical health and personal or critical autonomy. Built on this foundation of needs that everyone possesses, both individually and collectively, Doyal and Gough accept that there are intermediate needs that are relative to the circumstances in which people find themselves. Physical health needs are similar to the needs at the bottom end of Maslow's hierarchy, but autonomy is something different, which we would argue is crucial for an understanding of need as it relates to social work in the community.

Doyal and Gough (1991) see autonomy at two levels: personal and critical. First, *personal* autonomy is the minimum necessary level of human agency required for some degree of human dignity. It means the opportunity for personal agency and having a voice in decisions that affect one's life. For someone with learning difficulties, for instance, this would mean an opportunity to have a say in the important aspects of his/her life in the same way as any other citizen would, for example, what school to attend, where to live, who to have as friends, what leisure facilities to use and where to seek work. For people to be able to maximise the satisfaction of their needs, they require *critical* autonomy (Doyal and Gough, 1991; Dean, 2010). This degree of autonomy is necessary for people, individually and collectively, to 'question and to participate in *agreeing or changing* the rules' (Doyal and Gough, 1991, p 67). As Dean (2010) notes, this autonomy is not seen as an individualistic notion, but one that is fundamentally collective. In that sense critical autonomy reflects our notion of social work in the community, in which individuals and communities need their voices to be heard and their views considered and acted on if their needs are going to be met effectively. This is why the Doyal and Gough concept of critical autonomy is so important in informing a practice based on respect and empowerment in which the needs and strengths of individuals are understood to be linked inextricably with the strengths and needs of the communities within which they live. The other aspect of critical autonomy which is important to us here is that, in order to be effective, it requires people to be skilful and knowledgeable (Dean, 2010), in particular knowledgeable of different cultural and social opportunities from which they can make comparisons between their own and others' needs.

Although these three approaches to need assist in the assessment and explanation of the needs of individuals and communities, the theory of need presented by Doyal and Gough (1991) is most congruent with social work in the community as it considers individuals and their personal needs, collective needs and an ability to make comparisons between the needs of different people. Doyal and Gough's theory can be used in connection with Maslow's (1970) hierarchy of needs and Bradshaw's (1972) taxonomy of need by considering the need for physical health, which is congruent with Maslow's physiological needs, and exploring personal and critical autonomy, which are congruent with Bradshaw's felt, expressed and comparative needs. Including each of these aspects when considering need is crucial as individual and collective need should not be divided (Dean, 2010). When exploring and assessing individual need, collective need, either of a geographical area or of a collective community, must also be understood. For example, a social worker should attempt to understand the collective need of the Somali part of a local population of people with learning difficulties who live in a specific district. Likewise, the needs of a community or collective must recognise the accumulation of diverse and unique individual needs, as an assessment of need that only addresses the requirements of a generalised majority would have the effect of oppressing the marginalised minority. We argue, throughout this book, that the whole point of social work in the community is to hear the voices of communities and especially those individuals within the community who are often marginalised in order to avoid the predominance of more powerful voices such as those of politicians, managers and professionals (Doyal and Gough, 1991). It is this approach to need that reflects the sort of professional practice which we are calling 'social work in the community', and which we believe is more likely to make a difference to marginalised people's lives.

Anti-oppressive practice and social work in the community

Anti-oppressive practice is a critical component to social work practice with individuals and families and is equally important when working with communities. It seeks to acknowledge and combat the abuse of power by individuals, community establishments and society structures within society that lead to acts of racism, classism, sexism, heterosexism, ablism or ageism. Oppressive acts by these systems within society often lead to a restriction or blocking of resources, opportunities and needs to particular groups of individuals, often of a minority group, which leave the more powerful or dominant members of society with greater control and access to such resources, opportunities and services. Simply stated, oppression disadvantages some in favour of advantaging others, and thus limits the growth and development of those who are disadvantaged (Teater, 2010).

One way in which social workers can combat oppression is through anti-oppressive practice. Dominelli (1993, p 24) defined anti-oppressive practice as:

> [A] form of social work practice which addresses social divisions and structural inequalities in the work that is done with "clients" (users) or workers. Anti-oppressive practice aims to provide more appropriate and sensitive services by responding to people's needs regardless of their social status. Anti-oppressive practice embodies a person-centred philosophy, an egalitarian value system concerned with reducing the deleterious effects of structural inequalities upon people's lives; a methodology focusing on both process and outcome; and a way of structuring relationships between individuals that aims to empower users by reducing the negative effects of hierarchy in their immediate interaction and the work they do together.

Anti-oppressive practice is congruent with the strengths perspective and empowerment approach, as discussed above, where the social worker and service user work collaboratively to identify needs and goals and define, locate and use individual, interpersonal, community and societal strengths and resources to overcome blocked opportunities and resources.

Anti-oppressive practice can be considered in a number of ways when using social work in the community. First, it can be considered when identifying differences between community members and social workers. Social workers should be cognisant to the particular categories of people with whom they are working. For example, how will a white social worker be perceived when working with a black minority ethnic community, and how will this social worker perceive the community? Even if a social worker does share some commonalities with the community, she or he may still not fully understand the experiences and perspectives of that community. Therefore, social workers should be empathic to the community and attempt to solicit and understand their experiences and perspectives, particularly when they are seen as representing the more powerful or dominant members of the community or society (Twelvetrees, 2008). This can only be achieved through communication (verbal and non-verbal) and by taking a position of curiosity when working with the community, such as that discussed under social constructivism above.

Summary and conclusion

In this chapter we have looked in greater detail at what social work in the community might look like as a professional practice and the theories and methods to whoch social workers might use. The basic characteristics of systems approaches, social constructionism, the strengths perspective and empowerment approaches were discussed to illustrate particular theories and methods that social workers could incorporate into their practice in order to encourage the consideration of the community. Each of these theories or methods does not consider the individual alone but, rather, they consider the strengths and needs of individuals within their environments and how individual need is interdependent and interrelated to environmental or community need.

The chapter also explored the concept of need, which is an area that has been heavily used but poorly defined in policy and practice. We have argued for a more sophisticated understanding of this term so that social work practice that is designed to meet the needs of marginalised people can actually do so. The argument that 'need' is both individual and collective and that the two are inextricably linked is a helpful one. It undermines the habitual contemporary practice of many statutory agencies, which focus their attention purely on the individual without taking into account the broader social factors that explain and provide potential resources to meet the needs of that individual. Until social work can adopt this more integrated approach to understanding and meeting need it is unlikely to make a difference in people's lives.

We have also stressed Doyal and Gough's (1991) contention that there are aspects of human needs that are universal, and the most pertinent of these for our purposes are the concepts of personal and critical autonomy. Once again individual and collective needs are argued here as integral and mutually dependent. There is a collective notion of voice here that supports the practice of social work in the community that we explain in this book. Unless social work adopts this approach, enabling individuals and the communities within which they live to develop critical autonomy, the ability to be able to understand and comment on the rules that govern their lives, and indeed, to change those rules if necessary, then it is highly unlikely that their needs are going to be met effectively. While there has been a substantial increase in interest in involving service users (Beresford, 2003; DH, 2006) and communities (Stepney and Popple, 2008) in discussion and debate about service development, this is still at an early stage. Unless this practice, of hearing the collective and individual voices of people within communities, can become mainstream in organisations and broader social policy, then social work is unlikely to make a difference in people's lives.

Historical and legal context: development of social work in the community

Introduction

There is a long and strong tradition of considering 'community' in social work (Midgley, 1995; Payne, 2005; Stepney and Popple, 2008), and it is a tradition that made a reappearance from the late 1990s (Stepney and Popple, 2008) after a period of about 20 years in the wilderness. From 1979 until 1997 a Conservative government in the UK (it was much the same with other right-wing governments elsewhere in the world at the time) demonstrated an ideological resistance to the notion of community. This is reflected in the famous quotation from Margaret Thatcher while Prime Minister in the UK, 'There is no such thing as society. There are individual men and women, and there are families' (Thatcher, 1987). Although the New Labour government that came to power in 1997 largely continued Thatcherite policies in a number of areas of social welfare policy (Baldwin, 2002, 2008), as a government they did harbour a greater interest in the concept of community. At the time of writing this book, the current Coalition government is enhancing the focus on community through their discussions and promotions of the 'Big Society' and 'localism' agendas, which aims to give more power and control to local communities. The increasing emergence of community, particularly through policy agendas, has had an influence in the academic and policy worlds by reintroducing an interest in an exploration of the importance of community as theory and practice. We believe community is a concept that has some purchase for people in their everyday lives and is, therefore, regardless of the views of government, likely to re-emerge as a viable way of understanding diverse worlds.

The origins of community within social work

We begin this chapter by exploring the origins of community within social work. Readers who want to study the historical development of social work in any more depth need to look elsewhere (see, for example, Cree and Myers, 2008; Ferguson and Woodward, 2009; Burnham 2011; Wilson et al, 2011). One point worth noting from these sources is that social work, as we are aware of it in today's UK climate, originated from a number of different Christian religious streams, notably in Victorian Britain. Charitable organisations or friendly visiting societies (Cree and Myers, 2008) had been in existence for many years, but they were 'epitomised' (Burnham, 2011) by the Charity Organisation Society (COS), founded in 1869 by upper and middle-class Victorians. Like similar organisations, COS were concerned about the threat of lawlessness and insurrection from the working classes living in the large cities of the UK (Ferguson and Woodward, 2009). Their focus was on the 'deserving' poor who managed to avoid the workhouse, although Burnham (2011, p 8) argues that this distinction, between deserving and undeserving, was a bit of a myth. For instance, he cites examples of COS workers sticking with 'rogue' families against organisational policy.

The COS approach was an attempt to organise the great range of charitable giving in the UK in a way that encouraged the poor to take personal responsibility for their situation and to seek gainful employment in order to meet those responsibilities. The nascent social workers who were employed by COS started to develop what they termed scientific charity, where they assessed the relative merits of applicants and dispersed money only to those assessed as deserving of charity. COS was driven by this threat posed by the working class and a belief that their circumstances of poverty and deprivation were the result of their lower moral values. The aim of COS may have been to try and channel all applications for charity through their assessment process but, as Cree and Myers (2008, p 23) note, in 'practice, the COS never managed to exert the control it needed or wished over the voluntary societies or their service users'. Cree and Myers also discuss the legacy of COS, noting in particular the care and control functions of both the workhouse and COS. Despite the reputation of the former as largely about punishment and the latter as the forerunner to caring casework, the reality was more complicated than that, with COS workers exerting considerable leverage over working-class applicants' behaviour before they were eligible for charity (Cree and Myers, 2008).

The other movement, which sprang up at much the same time, was the Settlement movement. There was some overlap in membership of these two organisations that makes an attempt to separate them out problematic, however. While some involved in setting up the Settlement movement had concerns about the scientific method rooted in a strongly moralistic value base, Settlements had much the same motivation as COS, which was 'to promote social harmony through active citizenship' (Ferguson and Woodward, 2009, p 20). Their analysis of the causes of poverty and deprivation adopted a more socialist perspective, influenced as it was by the Fabian Society. Settlements were set up in working-class communities and brought young middle and upper-class university students to live in these communities for the purpose of mutual education. Young students placed in such communities were expected to bring their middle-class values to poor working-class families in order to educate them, while at the same time making use of the opportunity to gain some understanding of working-class life and the origins of poverty from first-hand experience.

In this context Hugman's (2009, pp 1138-9) claim that COS and Settlements could be seen as the 'beginnings of two broad strands of social work that can be seen running through the profession from then until the present day' is a little simplistic. This brief history is important, however, because it indicates that individualism in social work has a long history dating back to the friendly visiting societies of the Victorian era and even earlier. We can also see that a more collective perspective on social work problems and issues was recognised from the very early days of the profession. Therefore, even though the more individualistic, casework approach to social work has largely prevailed as the accepted approach to professional practice, there is another tradition which emphasises self-help, community organisation, social action and a collective approach to both the identification and addressing of social problems.

This historical interlude is also important because it indicates two different approaches to working-class communities, and the assessment of their difficulties and how they might be addressed. The casework approach, which emphasised the skills of assessing those who were deserving of charity, can be seen reflected in much of current local authority social work, for example, in adult services teams, where there is an emphasis on assessment and care management as the means for determining the eligibility entitlements of those referred to the organisation.

The legacy of the Settlement movement is reflected in the intermittent interest in community-based social work that has not really ever taken hold of the profession except at the periphery. Community work as practice and profession has been largely practised outside of mainstream social work (Stepney and Popple, 2008). Where it has become more to the forefront within the profession, areas that we look at in Chapters Four, Five, Six and Seven, practitioners have generally found the going tough, because their perspective on social problems has tended to be at the more radical end of the spectrum and marginalised from the mainstream.

Exercise box 3.1: Exploring the COS and Settlement movements

In pairs or small groups, discuss the following:

1. Why do you think casework became the mainstream approach to social work in the UK?
2. Why do you think the community development/community action version of social work from the Settlement movement did not become the mainstream?
3. What might social work look like now if the Settlement movement version had become the mainstream?
4. How effective would this be in tackling some of the social problems that social workers deal with?

We now turn to an examination of a number of concepts and ideas that reflect an interest in community in relation to social work. This involves looking at models and methods of practice that are, in the current organisational climate for social work employment, unlikely to be practised by qualified social workers. It is not our intention to argue here for one particular model of practice that ought to be or could be practised in, for example, local authority children and families or adult services teams. In the current real world of social work employment, we feel it is much more useful to look at social work in the community in a more general way as a key aspect of social work. Cree and Myers (2008), in the introductory book to this series, argue this point, which we would like to echo strongly here. Practising with the community context in mind when working with individuals is, we would argue, the most effective way of making a positive difference in people's lives. Some of the community-orientated traditions in social and community work have a great deal to helped a great deal in this context so we now spend some time briefly exploring what the history and development of these approaches have to teach us, before returning to three in particular (community social work, community development and community profiling) in subsequent chapters (Chapters Four, Five and Six respectively). The concepts reflected in the approaches we now explore are central to understanding our approach to social work in the community in the rest of the book.

We start by considering *social development*, as explained by Midgley (1995). He argues for community participation as a key aspect of this approach to social policy, and places social development at the forefront of state intervention in social welfare, with the aim being defined as 'to promote a proper adjustment between individuals and their communities' (Midgley, 1995, p 2). This approach to state intervention is based on an ideology that people have a collective right to control their own affairs. This is an argument that is fundamentally different to the neoliberal view that the best focus for welfare policy is on individual consumers within a market of care provision. Social development is reflected in much of the ideology about community (Powell, 1999) as argued by governments such as Tony Blair's New Labour. Midgley notes the tensions for the state in facilitating community participation for social development because there is a tendency for state control to be undermined if too much autonomy is given to communities to 'mobilise and help themselves' (Powell, 1999, p 8).

The main practice orientation for social development has been *community development* defined as 'helping groups come together and participate in gaining skills and confidence to promote services and facilities in their locality' (Payne, 2005, p 49). Most community development work tends to be within state-controlled parameters and was, under the New Labour government, a top-down process. An example includes 'Action Zones', which were created by the government to tackle poverty in targeted communities (Stepney and Popple, 2008). We note, however, Midgley's analysis that tensions between empowerment and state control arise when community development has a more radical edge, as it did with the Community Development Projects (CDPs) in the UK in the 1960 and 1970s (Stepney and Popple, 2008). These projects, introduced by a Labour government, were anti-poverty initiatives focused on specific communities across the UK in which there was evidence of considerable disadvantage. The distinctively radical edge that was developed by CDP workers was more akin to *community action*, defined as 'direct action often at a local level to change government or official policies and practices or attitudes of powerful groups ... often class-based' (Payne, 2005, p 49). Workers employed by the projects adopted a Marxist analysis, noting that it was the contradictions of capitalist economic production that led to poverty. The argument was that these contradictions related to the cycles of production and consumption that created unemployment and inequalities within the labour market and which had a disproportionate effect on the working class. Poverty was then the result of structural factors rather than individual fecklessness or the incompetence of people living in these communities (Ferguson et al, 2005; Baldwin, 2011).

The radical edge to community development can also be seen in the methods used. Clarke (2002, p 105) notes that 'community development is the process that puts ordinary people, as active and valued participants, into planning and delivering changes'. This is a problem for the state as it is very likely that this process will set up a 'challenge to the power of the traditional authorities' (p 107). Ferguson and Woodward (2009) note that within community development practice there is a very specific challenge to the power of the authorities to define what is a problem for the community.

It was the continual ability of CDPs to remind government that it was structural factors that were the root cause of poverty in the target areas that led largely to their demise within a few years (Loney, 1983; Mayo, 1994; Stepney and Popple, 2008).

Community development, as a practice, is fundamentally about facilitating the expression of power within communities. We have learned from the service user movement that social workers cannot empower individuals – they can only enable people to realise their own power (Evans, 1997; Beresford, 2003; Baldwin and Sadd, 2006) – and we would argue it is much the same with communities. By providing groups within communities with the skills that they require to engage in participatory processes, community development can facilitate this process of empowerment. The concepts of power and politics are very important here, as many of the communities that community workers engage with can be characterised as displaced from political processes. Empowerment, through the opportunity to engage in political processes, is, then, one of the goals of community development. The concept of need was discussed in Chapter Two and in particular the definition of need from the seminal work on the concept by Doyal and Gough (1991), who argue that there are universal needs that cut across culture, geography and circumstance. Apart from the need for food and shelter, they argue that critical autonomy is a basic and universal human need. Unless individuals and communities can have a degree of autonomy or 'voice' in decisions that are made about services to meet their needs, it is likely that other more powerful voices will dominate, and it will be politicians, managers and professionals whose perspectives prevail. The critical aspect of autonomy is crucial because, Doyal and Gough argue, communities need to have the ability to make sense of the knowledge and values that are informing policy developments. Community education, as argued by Freire (1996), involves raising the consciousness (conscientisation) of working-class communities so that they can have a more powerful voice in the development of policy and practice that fundamentally affects their lives. Alinsky (1971) argues a similar approach in ensuring communities have the information and understanding to engage in community organising and radical community action. Community development, therefore, by providing voice, ensures that traditional power positions are questioned and challenged. Social or community workers engaged in community development have this role of community education, enabling communities to develop critical autonomy and voice in their struggles with those in power.

Community work has provided a rich literature of practice-based material (see, for example, Twelvetrees, 2008) that has detailed the skills of working in community settings. Skills in community needs assessment or community profiling, group work, networking, community and group advocacy, project management and social planning are all described in detail in Chapters Four,

Five and Six. These skills and their potential applicability to a huge range of organisations, settings and professionals and non-professional practitioners are generalised in a helpful manner in this literature, although there is little attempt to connect the practice of community work to professional social work practice. We come back to look at some of these skills in Chapters Four, Five and Six.

Community social work is an approach that was developed from the review of social work carried out in the 1980s. The report that was produced by the Barclay Committee has become known as the Barclay Report (1982), which is described as an attitude of mind rather than a blueprint for action, and it may be this lack of specific structure that resulted in it never being put into practice in any concerted way, apart from in some small-scale projects (Smale and Bennett, 1989; Darvill and Smale, 1990). The Barclay Committee noted that most care and support for people comes from family, friends and neighbours within their local community so, in order to maintain people living in those communities, the most effective focus for practice would be to provide formal support to community networks and resources. This report followed on from the Seebohm Report (1970) that also argued that the new social services departments should reflect the nature of the communities that they served.

One of the key features of community social work is the 'development of flexible decentralised patterns of organisation' (Barclay Committee, 1982, p 198). This was interpreted in some of the pilot projects as 'patch-based social services' (Beresford, nd), with the emphasis on partnership between the local state and citizens 'focusing more closely on the community and its strengths' (Barclay Committee, 1982, p 198). This was seen as important in enabling social workers and social services to deliver more effective services (Smale and Bennett, 1989). Practice, in these patch-based teams, was to be 'directed more to the support and strengthening of informal networks, to caring for the carers and less to the rescue of casualties when networks fail' (Barclay Committee, 1982, p 200). In this way, community social work emphasises prevention rather than dealing with acute crisis work. The belief was that such an approach would reduce the requirement to deal with crisis work.

There was evidence of positive effects from this approach in some of the pilot and evaluation projects (Smale and Bennett, 1989; Darvill and Smale, 1990); however, there were also problems. The Barclay Report noted that not all communities were benign and that some individuals could be a 'serious social menace' (Barclay Committee, 1982, p 212) and would continue to require resources for their own or other people's protection. This admission rather undermined the notion that this was the way to deliver social services, especially as the evidence of prevention was not as well documented as it might have been. What literature there is (Smale and Bennett, 1989; Darvill and Smale, 1990) provides more assertion than evidence, even if there is evidence of services being positively welcomed by people in patch areas.

In order to realise this approach to service delivery, which was heavily echoed in the transformation agenda for adult services under New Labour (DH, 2007), what would be required was a major shift in political, managerial and professional will, not to mention an investment in prevention during the period that acute crisis work reduces (assuming the theory is correct). This would indeed be a paradigm change (Baldwin, 2008) if it were to be enacted. Other criticisms include the failure of the Barclay Committee to properly define terms such as 'community' and 'community social work' that allowed many people and organisations to claim they were already doing it (see Thomas, 1983). Thomas also criticises Barclay for failing to take resource implications seriously. The cost of maintaining crisis services while building prevention services meant that the plans were largely doomed to failure with an incoming Thatcher government intent on cutting back on public expenditure.

Despite the Barclay Report, which was commissioned by the previous Labour administration, what the Thatcher government of the 1980s actually developed was *community care*, and it is that aspect of social work in the community that we need to address. Several authors (see, for example, Heenan, 2004; Jordan, 2007; Stepney and Popple, 2008) note the link between Seebohm, Barclay and Griffiths, with the latter in particular arguing that community social work was the best way of putting the community care changes he proposed into practice. This continuity of policy advice through the 1960s, 1970s and 1980s is fascinating. Community social work, with the additional practice of care management as a way of organising and managing community services, was what Griffiths recommended, but this aspect of his advice was swiftly dumped in favour of care management and, especially, financial or resource management as the central facets of the 'community care revolution' (Audit Commission, 1992). Community care, therefore, has never reflected an ideology of 'care in the community' let alone social work in the community.

The last area that we want to mention is *community needs assessment* or *community profiling*. This practice is described, defined and analysed in great detail by Hawtin and Percy-Smith (2007). They provide a list of reasons for communities or organisations to carry out community profiles, including assessing the needs or wants of a community, whether it be a geographical area or a community of interest; evaluating whether a community's needs are being met; identifying trends in service requirements; mapping existing services and how they meet expressed needs; evaluating service delivery; providing information for fundraising; listening to the expressed needs of a community and improving relationships with people who use services; encouraging involvement by the community; and promoting understanding of the organisation and being accountable to service users (Hawtin and Percy-Smith, 2007, p 13). Community profiles have been used in detail by public sector bodies, but seldom by social workers, however. The approach is much more to do with resource and social care planning, with a small degree of community consultation. On Arnstein's (1969) ladder of participation, such practice rarely gets beyond the tokenistic stage of consultation. Perhaps using the pun intended in the radical social work collective of the 1970s (Case Con), we could call this con-sultation.

We return to community profiling practice in Chapter Six, but now turn to the recent policy and statutory context in order to explore current opportunities for social work practice in the community.

Context of government policy and rhetoric

Children in need

Section 17(10) of the Children Act 1989 in England and Wales places a legal requirement on local authorities to identify and assist children in need. Part of this statutory duty requires local authorities to map the needs of children and young people across the authority's area of responsibility. This means collecting or using information to make aggregate estimations of the needs of young people who fit the 'in need' category so that appropriate services can be provided to meet those needs. This has clearly been problematic for local authorities, and some observations suggest that local authorities have generally failed to identify children in need in any systematic way (Axford, 2010).

This process, for assessing children in need generally across a local authority area, requires the authority to collect data on a range of health-related and socioeconomic factors in order to identify the needs and develop services to meet such needs. Axford (2010) notes that most local authorities use data from the aggregation of need as revealed in statistics collected from current cases. As he mentions, but does not pursue, this merely measures current demand, not need. To make evaluations of needs across a whole population, it would be necessary to look at need on a collective basis and to start with need rather than those already receiving a service. The latter approach could, of course, miss out sections of the community not currently receiving a service because of a whole range of factors such as institutionalised racism or communities marginalised by other social processes. It would also be necessary to conduct detailed community profiles to determine needs as defined not just by welfare professionals but also by the community themselves (Hawtin and Percy-Smith, 2007).

In order for local authorities to collect this information, they need to carry out mapping exercises. The guidance is very specific about the need for local authorities to work in a participatory way with children and young people as well as with their parents in order for their voices to be heard in any evaluation of needs and requirements. This puts these mapping exercises firmly in the realms of a community profile (Hawtin and Percy-Smith, 2007) that is based on such partnerships with communities. Such exercises are clearly a statutory requirement for planning and development purposes but they are also important for practitioners who can use the information that emerges to make comparative evaluations of individuals in need in relation to the needs of the general population. (We discuss the rationale and the methods for carrying out community profiles in Chapter Six.)

The *Framework for the assessment of children in need* is the system required to assess the needs of individual children identified as being 'in need'. According to government guidance on the assessment of children in need (DH et al, 2000, p 17), there are three areas or 'interrelated systems or domains' for such an assessment. These are: the child's developmental needs, parenting capacity and, the third side of the triangle, family and environmental factors. This guidance is a clear recognition that, when assessing someone's needs (in this case a child in need and his or her family), it is not good enough to focus only on their individual and immediate family circumstances.

The framework is quite specific in arguing that these environmental factors are an important part of building a picture of the needs and strengths of children in need. The argument states that all family members are influenced in positive and negative ways by 'the neighbourhood and social networks in which they live' (DH et al, 2000, p 22). Therefore, factors such as employment, income, social integration (including experience of racism or other forms of marginalisation) and community resources should all be taken into consideration in assessing need. In addition, the guidance (DH, 2000, p 13) stresses the importance of understanding the 'contribution of the community in providing practical and emotional support to the immediate family'. Problems with a 'hostile neighbourhood' (p 14) are also seen as potentially important. How a social worker goes about assessing these factors is an interesting question, and one for which this book should help find answers.

Community care

Changes made in the 1990s as a result of Conservative government policy were largely ideological (Baldwin, 2008). The major changes that took place involved the introduction of a market in care by separating assessment of the needs of individuals from the provision of those services. Commissioning of services and assessment have been retained as residual roles for local authorities while the provision of services has been largely privatised to external providers, in the private, voluntary and, in a very few cases, service user-led sectors.

It is interesting to note, however, that the report commissioned by the government to look into changes in the way that adult services were organised in the 1980s, led by Sir Roy Griffiths, actually emphasised the importance of a community orientation to the delivery of services. The Griffiths Report followed the logical arguments of the Seebohm Report of 1968 that led to the establishment of social services departments in the early 1970s, and Griffiths even argued that his recommendations required the implementation of community social work as expounded in the Barclay Report (1982; see above and Chapter Four for further discussion of this approach).

There was a statutory requirement in the legislation that followed the publication of the White Paper *Caring for people: Community care in the next decade and beyond* (DH, 1989) that local authorities consult with the communities that they served. The resulting data, reflecting the expressed needs of that population, was seen as a key source of information for the community care plans they were required to publish. Apart from this statutory requirement, however, community care changes in the 1990s were largely focused on individual need. The opportunity to look at individuals in their communities was there in a vaguely rhetorical way and did find its way into some of the guidance, notably that produced by the National Institute for Social Work (NISW, 1983), which had championed community social work in the years since Barclay. What we have since then has remained much the same (Baldwin, 2008), with the firm establishment of service users as individuals within a quasi-market of care over which they have little control (Ferguson and Woodward, 2009).

Our health, our care, our say and *Putting people first* – these New Labour government initiatives that came as a result of a substantial public consultation exercise – culminated in a rhetorical position for the New Labour government. There was substantial support for patients and service users to have choice and control over services and for those services to be provided close to people's own homes.

The concept of personalisation has been developed by non-service user organisations and politicians from their interpretation of the philosophy of independent living and the idea of 'direct payments', which emerged from the disability and service user movements (Beresford and Croft, 1984). While personalisation, on the one hand, and independent living and direct payments, on the other, derive from a belief that service users should have more control over the resources that they require to meet their expressed needs, it is the case that the policy of personalisation has become more rhetoric than reality for many service users. However, in principle, personalisation should enable service users to express personal autonomy over their care, both with respect to their voice being considered in assessment and in the services that will be provided to meet those needs.

As Doyal and Gough have noted (1991), the concept of critical autonomy requires people to be able to develop a critical appreciation of their circumstances and ways of meeting their needs. However, for people who have experienced marginalisation and discrimination for most of their lives, this is not going to come easily. Organisations such as People First (Ferguson and Woodward, 2009) have provided mutual aid to people with learning difficulties that has enabled them to learn how to use opportunities for choice and control through collective approaches to autonomy, sometimes referred to as 'speaking up'. If service users are going to be able to make use of the service user version of personalisation, they are going to have to know or learn how to ensure their voices are heard. Collective experience of disability is likely to marginalise individuals, and a collective approach to autonomy – collective voice and mutual aid, in other words – would seem to be essential.

How this service user-inspired approach to service provision was interpreted by government, however, was as the 'personalisation agenda' (DH, 2007), which, rather than facilitating anything resembling collective autonomy, effectively cemented the position of service users as individuals within a market of care. In addition, with tightening eligibility requirements, people who are entitled to services are likely to be in substantial or critical need before they get a service. It is increasingly the case that individualised assessment for services results in individual rather than collective service provision (Ferguson and Woodward, 2009). Lastly, the context of austerity and cutbacks to services, under the current Coalition government in the UK, means that the rhetoric that personalisation provides choice and control to individuals, let alone to people experiencing collective marginalisation within society as a result of ageism or disabling attitudes, begins to look distinctly optimistic.

As resources to meet need are individualised through personalisation, the community-based services that used to be provided, problematic though they may have been in some cases, are consequently less likely to be there. Eligibility criteria will deny people needing services to maintain them in the community from getting access to them, and throw them back onto the mercy of friends, family and neighbours, with little in the way of support for service users or carers to prevent networks from breaking down.

Strong and prosperous communities – there are more general 'community development'-orientated policy documents and initiatives that New Labour pursued in the latter years of their administration. These indicate a renewed interest in the concept of community following 18 years of Conservative government, in which the dominant ideology was of individualism, most notably reflected in Thatcher's comment that there was no such thing as society, only individuals and families (Thatcher, 1987).

These initiatives appear to reflect an interest in the context of community and the degree to which this is important to people. The concept of community development or community capacity building (see Chapter Five for a more detailed discussion of these concepts), suggests that the New Labour government wanted to develop community cohesion and community resources in order to improve the well-being of both the community and the individuals who live within them. We look in more detail later at the concept of community, but it is interesting to note the philosophical difference between a belief that only individuals exist (let alone matter) and the concept that communities can have 'well-being' or 'cohesion'.

The White Paper *Strong and prosperous communities* (CLG, 2006) was interesting because it appeared to marry up a concern for community development with the transformation of community services which was another New Labour government agenda (DH, 2007). It starts by arguing that people will be 'given more control over their lives; consulted and involved in running services' (CLG, 2006, p 2). It explains that they will 'encourage councils to develop neighbourhood charters setting out local standards and priorities, and to take opportunities to manage services' at the level of the neighbourhood' (CLG, 2006, p 2). There is also a concern to enhance 'community cohesion', recognising that there are some areas where there are particular challenges.

Therefore, is this and other New Labour policy, a reflection of an interest in the importance of community to ordinary citizens as suggested in the rhetoric, or is it something else? For the purposes of our discussion here, about the policy drivers to consider community as an important part of a social work service delivery, this policy is a key factor, although we also need to look at the current Coalition government's 'Big Society' policy to see what happens next. The previous New Labour government clearly linked community development and community cohesion with a belief that it was through citizen involvement in their communities that services, such as those provided by social workers, would be transformed. The rhetoric on the policy of transformation was that it would result in people getting 'choice over the services they receive, influence over those who provide them, and higher service standards' (CLG, 2006, p 2).

To be more analytical and sceptical, we need to note that New Labour maintained the focus of service provision on individuals as consumers of services in a continuing privatised market (Baldwin, 2008; Ferguson and Woodward, 2009). It is hard to see how an interest in community can be married, philosophically, with an interest in extending market forces within welfare service development.

'Big Society'

Reading much of the policy documentation from the Conservative Party and from the Coalition agreement, plus the rhetoric from David Cameron's regular relaunching of this major policy initiative, it is easy to see the continuity between New Labour's approach to communities and the Conservative's 'Big Society'. The themes are similar – under the 'Big Society' there will be a redistribution of power from the central state to local communities and individuals, a recognition of the importance of communities taking responsibility for their well-being, stimulation of local community action, provision of transparent information for local people to make choices, enabling the third sector (and indeed private enterprise) to deliver services in local communities and encouraging social enterprises by providing financial resources to local communities to deliver services. The 'Big Society' envisions much that has been delivered by public services in the past being delivered by voluntary organisations and private enterprise, with local communities making the decisions about the services they want and who will deliver them.

Wells (2011) argues that the 'Big Society' is similar to the New Labour approach except that the former is more explicitly about the withdrawal of the state. It is hard to divorce 'Big Society' policy from the Coalition government's policy on cutting the deficit by reducing state expenditure across the board to a degree not seen since the creation of the welfare state. Indeed, Wells (2011, p 52) argues, 'the rationale for the Big Society poses a considerable threat to the post-war welfare state'. Much of the immediate commentary on 'Big Society' policy (see, for example, Coote, 2010; Wells, 2011; Lawless, 2011) has noted that it is a policy based more on populism than evidence or, as Lawless (2011, p 56) puts it, it is a policy based on 'fashionable populist polemic, informing a "common sense" perspective on society'. However, the selective use of evidence where it is used, notably ignoring the evidence that regeneration of communities requires sustained long-term public funding, suggests that government policy is driven more by the need to cut public expenditure than to improve the lot of marginalised communities. The news that charities, and particularly charities providing services to children in need, are in a 'fight for survival' (Ramesh, 2011) in the face of public expenditure cuts pulls the rug from under that pillar of 'Big Society' that is voluntary sector provision.

Coote (2010) picks up a number of themes of the 'Big Society' policy and engages them in some critical scrutiny. In relation to the theme of taking personal responsibility for community action, she notes that 'not everyone has the same capacity to help themselves and others.[...] People who have least will benefit least from the transfer of power and responsibility, whilst those with higher stocks of social and economic resources will be better placed to seize the new opportunities' (Coote, 2010, p 3). Coote also notes that voluntary work takes time, and those who are 'poor in discretionary time' (2010, p 3), who are working long hours on low wages, are unlikely to be able to participate in the same way as others with more of such resources. Her overall analysis is that the 'Big Society', as a policy, falls down because of its failure to address 'the economic causes of poverty and inequality. It pays no attention to forces within modern capitalism that leads to accumulations of wealth and power in the hands of the few at the expense of the others' (2010, p 3). A 'Big Society' policy that made social justice the main goal, and extended running local services to the economy so that local people could have more democratic control of the economy as well, might make a difference. Coote also argues that 'co-production' (2010, p 7), or user involvement, should be the 'standard way of getting things done'. This would provide a far better context for community empowerment than merely shunting the 'doing it' culture from the public sector to the business and third sector.

Summary and conclusion

In this chapter we have looked at the history of social work and the twin traditions of individualised casework and community action that developed from Christian religion-inspired charity work in Victorian Britain. We have noted that it is the individualism reflected in the work of organisations such as COS that has predominated in contemporary social work as practised in mainly statutory settings. The tradition of community action, community education and community development persists, however. This enables us to track the development of an alternative view to individualist casework – social work in the community. This perspective on social work has a long tradition in the history of social work as a developing profession. Although it has seldom broken through into the mainstream of professional social work practice, there is much within that history to commend the knowledge, skills and values of a community approach to contemporary professional practice, even in crisis-driven teams.

We have also traced the development of more recent policy development, noting how 'community' came back in fashion under New Labour's approach to communities, and has continued in the Conservative notion of 'Big Society' within the Coalition government. We argue that these policies provide an imperative to pursue a community perspective on practice. While we might fear that policy is little more than rhetoric in the context of government debt, global recession and the worst cuts in public services seen in the post-war period, it is the government's case that a more community-orientated, service user-led and preventive service is not just more efficient, effective and economical, but it is also what the citizens of our communities are wanting. Unless we push at this apparently open door as a profession, we will never know whether it was rhetoric or held an element at least of reality.

Those interested in seeing individuals within their community contexts, and those who believe the ills of working-class communities are largely constructed by the inequalities created by capitalism, can use these policy contexts to practise in more collective ways. In subsequent chapters we link that tradition and the current policy framework to illustrative examples as we begin to build a picture of what an alternative professional practice might look like. This is a radical practice that we argue will make a positive difference to people's lives.

In the following chapters we expand on our explanation of what social work in the community is by looking in more detail at three approaches already mentioned – community social work, community development and community profiling. We start once more from illustrative examples, exploring what is expected of social workers and students in the way of knowledge, skills and values for effective professional practice, and then use the information to analyse the examples.

Practice example 1: Jenny

Jenny is a social worker based in a community team for people with learning difficulties and she has long recognised the way people with learning difficulties are often pushed to the outside of society. She has seen how they are often not told of important things that are happening and which could make a difference to their lives, and are seldom asked to express their views. She has worked effectively with individuals for 10 years, in a person-centred way, acting as an advocate and supporter to enable service users to take more control of their lives. She and her colleagues were initially excited by the prospect of the personalisation agenda as it seemed to mark a move away from the provision of emergency services to community resources that would prevent emergencies and enable people to choose and control the support they needed and received. What she finds is that resources are still scarce and people only get a service when everything else has fallen apart. Many service users she comes across don't know about personalisation and what it is supposed to involve. What can Jenny and her colleagues do to avoid being sucked into ever more emergency work, and actually practise within their professional values?

Practice example 2: Hasan and Geoffrey

One of the people Hasan works with in the community mental health team is Geoffrey. Geoffrey came from Zimbabwe as a refugee and has since been given leave to stay and become a British citizen. He was a physiotherapist in Zimbabwe but has been unable to practise his profession in the UK because he was not able to bring the documentation out of Zimbabwe that would demonstrate his qualifications. He has worked in the care sector on the minimum wage, but, because of his reaction to the violence he experienced in Zimbabwe that was diagnosed as post-traumatic stress disorder (PTSD), he has been unable to work for six months. As well as spending a great deal of time ruminating about the past, Geoffrey also experiences flashbacks about the violence he suffered himself and saw meted out to others, including his father, who was killed in front of him. This causes him extreme anxiety resulting in panic attacks and his inability to self-organise. He lost his permanent residence and was forced to move to a different town, away from friends and family (he has a sister but she and her husband and children live 100 miles away). The severe symptoms from his PTSD brought him to the attention of Hasan's team. How can social work in the community help Hasan understand Geoffrey's position and begin to meet his needs?

Introduction

In the previous chapter we looked briefly at the history and development of some of the key models and methods for working with communities. In this and the following two chapters we aim to look in more detail at three of these methods so that we can learn what might be useful, appropriate and effective as forms of practice for contemporary social work in a range of settings. We also want to see what might be more effective practice if we, as social workers, want to make a difference in people's lives. There is evidence (Jones, 2005) that social workers are not happy with the kind of practice foisted on them by managerialist organisations, which are more concerned with managing resources than facilitating imaginative, creative professional practice. We look at the knowledge, skills and values of these approaches in specific relation to the above two practice examples. This chapter looks at community social work, as envisaged by the Barclay Report (Barclay, 1982) and built on in a number of pilot projects since.

We begin by looking in some detail at the definition and actual practice of community social work, focusing primarily on practice implications. We then revisit the two practice examples and address the consequences of using this model of practice for Jenny and Hasan as practitioners. Finally, we note the additional implications for professional social work practice in contemporary social work organisations.

The two illustrative examples of Jenny and Hasan are from a more individual or casework tradition in social work. We have chosen to look at these because it is in these areas of work where the imperative to work with an individual focus is most pressing, given the structure of policy, organisation and practice guidance within social services organisations, especially in the statutory sector. These examples should then provide us with the greater challenge of defining and describing social work in the community.

Community social work in practice

As stated in the previous chapter, the literature on community social work does rather shy away from being specific on the matter of practice, preferring to see it as a way of thinking rather than as a blueprint for action (Barclay Committee, 1982). In their concluding comments to their chapter on community social work, Stepney and Popple (2008, p 131) argue that for social workers to travel 'into the cold and troubled side of the community and grapple with a complex array of messy problems and everyday realities', they will need to remind themselves, above all, of the importance of critical thinking, the connections between theory and practice and a commitment to social justice. They argue that this knowledge, particularly these values, is 'more important than reliance on any specific technical skills' (p 131). While values underpinning practice are clearly essential there are, in the community social work literature, some pointers to what actual day-to-day practice might look like.

The Barclay Report lists a number of key aspects of practice. The first of these is partnership with other agencies and, most importantly, with communities themselves. In order for community social work to be effective, statutory services need to work in collaboration with 'informal caring networks and not in isolation from them' (Barclay Committee, 1982, p 201). Smale and Bennett (1989, p 11) refer to the importance of working in partnership with 'natural helping networks', so we can see both the imperative for partnership working and also the range of somewhat confusing terminology that is used (such as neighbourhoods, communities and networks).

In much the same way that contemporary good practice guidance talks about the importance of involving service users in service development, Barclay (1982, p 201) argues that communities should be able to contribute their experience to decisions on how resources are used as 'citizens who give and receive services should have opportunities to share in decisions that affect their lives'. What is different about the Barclay rhetoric in relation to contemporary rhetoric on involvement and consultation is the emphasis on *collective* voice rather than a focus on service users as individual consumers in a market of care. The practice skills involved in this work involve enabling, empowering, supporting and encouraging social networks, rather than taking over their caring role.

Barclay, and indeed other writers arguing for community approaches to social work (see, for example, Midgley and Livermore, 2005), strenuously argue for community social work to be informed by a clearly articulated knowledge base, which is both theoretical and practical. Midgley and Livermore (2005, p 153) argue that community social work requires better theory to 'embrace the effectiveness of practice'. Barclay (1982) argues for community social workers to have good theoretical knowledge that explains individuals in their community contexts. In addition, Barclay, supported by others writing specifically about community social work (see, for example, Hargreaves, 1982; Smale and Bennett, 1989) argues that knowledge of the local community is of central importance. Indeed, Hargreaves (1982) reminds us that this is one of the important things that service users want from their social workers.

Good community social work practice would also include counselling skills to be used for making assessments of individuals' needs and also in enabling them to accept a service. Barclay saw these skills, which would appear to be more akin to individual casework, as important because some individuals, in the early stages of dealing with social problems, will find it harder to acknowledge and accept that they have difficulties, and that a little help now might prevent a lot of trouble at a later stage. Counselling skills such as motivational approaches (Teater, 2010) could, therefore, be used for preventive purposes.

Community social work practice should involve skills in negotiating, bargaining, advocacy and signposting. Advocacy skills would suggest doing things for people and, indeed, community social work might well involve negotiating decision-making processes on behalf of individuals or groups within a community, but the principle should be one of enabling and empowerment, in which providing access to information is seen as a key aspect of empowerment. This is in direct opposition to a professional approach of mystification (Parsloe, 1983), in which practitioners keep hold of important knowledge in order to shore up their position of power. These skills may also involve aspects of community education (Freire, 1996) in which the professional practitioner teaches people how to negotiate decision-making systems so that they can do this for themselves rather than being reliant on professional advocacy to access services.

A key aspect of community social work in the original Barclay Report version, and in the literature evaluating the pilot projects, is the importance of ensuring that decisions are made at as low and local a point in the organisation as possible. While this might seem more to do with the organisation and management of services, there are also implications for social work practice. In order for a team to be able to make decisions about priorities for service delivery, they must have good local knowledge of their communities. This means that social work teams must have good links with other statutory agencies, with voluntary organisations and other service providers, as well as the informal networks in neighbourhoods, where, as the Barclay Report notes, the overwhelming amount of caring takes place (Barclay Committee, 1982). Priority decisions are political decisions in the sense that it is a political decision whether one individual or one community is given access to scarce resources rather than another (Baldwin, 2011). If social workers and their managers are going to make such decisions, then they need to be informed by the views of the local community they affect, at the very least. Even better, the argument goes, the local community should be involved in the decision.

In Chapter Six we argue that community profiling is a very powerful tool for social workers to use in order to learn more about the communities to which they are providing services. Knowing your neighbourhood or community is a key aspect of the knowledge necessary to practise community social work (Barclay Committee, 1982; Smale and Bennett, 1989; Hawtin and Percy-Smith, 2007); therefore, teams need to carry out or commission a community profile so that they can build this crucial knowledge and network of relationships. In order to be able to put these skills of community social work into practice, social workers and their managers need to have the autonomy to engage with, and negotiate, the provision of services to those local communities. This form of professional autonomy has largely been crushed by authoritarian managerialism, but is clearly necessary if social workers are going to be able to develop their knowledge and skills in community social work.

Barclay (1982, p 221) suggests four requirements for effective community social work, which include the following:

1. *Being accessible to local networks* Community social work was also known in some variations as 'patch-based social work' and it is argued that local presence, visibility and accessibility are as important as knowledge of the community by the team. Hence community social work teams were often placed in health centres or other community resources so that social workers could both see and be seen in the communities they served.

2. *Responsive and flexible* Clearly social workers are required to work within the statutory framework but there should be, the argument goes, flexibility within these confines for social workers to discover what local priorities are, and to address those within statutory parameters.

3. *Involvement in social planning and the provision of resources to meet newly identified needs* This was an idea built into the community care changes of the 1980s in which community consultation, community profiling and the systematic collection of data related to unmet needs would ensure that services were responsive to locally identified needs. It has been argued (Doyal and Gough, 1991; Hawtin and Percy-Smith, 2007) that providing communities with opportunities to have their voices heard in service development is central to any attempts to ensure that real needs are met. Responsibility for service development has tended to rest in the upper echelons of social services organisations. Community social work suggests that the responsibility for this should lie at all levels,

and social workers should be equally active in the identification and development of services, statutory, voluntary or informal, which meet the identified and expressed needs of local communities.

4. *Good working knowledge of people, groups and communities, versus restricted knowledge only about individuals* While this might seem a rather obvious point, the predominance of individualism (Plant, 1974), the focus of service delivery on individuals and the policy rhetoric of personalisation that sees potential service users as atomised consumers of care services, all suggest that these are arguments, as Hamlet would say, 'more honoured in the breach'. Community social workers need to be able to understand and identify with the communities they work within. This implies important underlying knowledge about theory as well as practical responses such as local knowledge and community presence.

Smale and Bennett (1989), evaluating community social work projects a few years on from the Barclay Report, came up with a number of similar skills that community social workers should be able to employ, but added two very specific ones, the first of which was group work. Smale and Bennett argued that much of what was necessary in community social work practice involved working with groups, formally and informally, and, if social workers were going to be proficient in this work, they needed to know about group dynamics and how to facilitate effective group processes. The second area that they were keen to stress was the importance of workload management to ensure there was space for community social workers to be flexible, imaginative and responsive in their approach to expressed community needs. While this would seem to be a management issue and one for social work in any setting, we argue that all social workers have a responsibility to make use of good supervision to ensure their workload is managed. Where a team is trying to avoid getting dragged into reactive crisis casework and to focus more on enabling and empowering people to make use of informal support networks, using a preventive approach, workload management is a crucial practice tool that social workers, with their managers, are responsible for using.

Exercise box 4.1: Whatever happened to community social work?

In pairs or small groups, discuss the following:

1. What might be some of the advantages of closer links between social work agencies and community/service user organisations, (a) for social workers and (b) for service users? Are there any disadvantages?

2. What are the main barriers to developing a community social work approach within statutory social work agencies, and how might these barriers be overcome?

3. Identify one or two steps that could contribute to the development of a community social work approach where you work or have worked.

Note: This exercise was adapted from one developed by colleagues at the University of Stirling for social workers working in predominantly statutory organisations, plus academic social workers, in a day seminar entitled 'Whatever happened to community social work in 2009?'.

Community social work ideas in action

We now return to Jenny and Hasan and their colleagues to see how the knowledge, skills and values we have just laid out might help inform their practice in their specific circumstances. Jenny and her colleagues want to avoid getting sucked ever more into crisis work in their community team for people with learning difficulties. Personalisation is supposed to be giving the people who use their service more in the way of choice and control over their lives, but in many instances the eligibility threshold is so high that service users have to be in crisis before they get a service. What are the issues then that arise for Jenny, if she is thinking more broadly than just a succession of individual people in need? What practical help can community social work offer her as she responds to the needs of service users in a more collective way? A collective approach would avoid seeing people as atomised individuals, endeavouring to understand them within the networks of their friends, family and neighbours that they encounter on a daily or weekly basis.

Hasan is dealing with someone who has very particular personal difficulties, so what can community social work do to help him enable Geoffrey to take back control in his life? What are the issues that are involved here? Geoffrey is experiencing symptoms of extreme distress which are causing difficulties in his local community, to the point where he has had to move far away from friends, family and the familiarity of his neighbourhood. Hasan could just see Geoffrey as another individual requiring resources to prop up his ailing independence while the mental illness is treated, or is there another way of looking at Geoffrey? Is there an approach to practice that would take into account the broader circumstances? In this case, and in Jenny's situation, how could we use some of the practical ideas listed above so that Jenny and Hasan might be able to understand and address these situations in a more collective and community-orientated manner? What is the knowledge that would inform community social work in this case? What are the skills involved for Hasan as he tries to tackle Geoffrey's difficulties? What are the values that underpin this broader and, we would argue, more effective way of dealing with individuals' problems?

Based on these questions, we now turn to the practice of community social work through Jenny and Hasan's experience, grappling with the problems of crisis work. But before we do this it is important to remind ourselves of the contested nature of the basic concepts of community and need. This is important because the way in which we understand such concepts determines the way in which we subsequently deal with them. There are sociological arguments here about discourse and the social construction of meaning and reality. The concept of discourse (Payne, 2005) defines the powerful ways of understanding that determine our reality. For instance, if government starts from an ideological position such as that within the quotation from Margaret Thatcher which we looked at in Chapter Three and, therefore believe that community is not an important consideration in addressing people's needs, then government is not likely to put resources into supporting communities. Indeed, this is what happened in communities such as those in South Wales where community well-being was closely linked to employment in the coal and steel industries. When government policy in the 1980s led to the demise of these industries, very little in the way of resources were put into the communities to redress the balance – people were expected to deal with the difficulties of unemployment and to support their families on an individual basis. A collective view of social work practice would take these structural factors into consideration and adopt a practice that addresses the collective results in working-class communities.

In our field of social services we have had a dominant ideology of individualism. The Tory governments under Thatcher and then Major, and continued under New Labour (Baldwin, 2008), have operated from a belief in the efficacy of market forces and competition in providing quality, choice and economy in delivering services. We have had such a system for 30 years now, so it is not surprising that social workers tend to think of service users and their needs within this individualistic frame of reference (Jordan, 2007). The reality of service users' day-to-day lives has not changed, but the ideology or discourse of individualism has meant that it is less likely that social workers will consider the holistic needs of service users in their communities and support networks.

The focus now is far more on entitlement to services (that is, eligibility) (Jordan, 2007; Ferguson and Woodward, 2009) than on this broader context of people living in communities and in networks of supportive relationships with potential resources at hand, such as transport systems, child minders, local hospitals, shops or employment. Of course the lack of these kinds of resources brings problems for people that are not of their own making. Lack of reasonable employment, for instance, creates poverty in whole communities. It is this sort of collective experience that service users are living with that social work in the community takes heed of when making sense of people's lives and constructing mechanisms of support for them.

Jenny

The question we are asking on Jenny's behalf is, what can she and her colleagues do to avoid being sucked into ever more emergency work and actually practise within their professional values? What can our understanding of community, needs and the knowledge, skills and values inherent within community social work provide to help in addressing this question?

First, it would be helpful for Jenny and her team to think about the nature of the communities involved. There is the community of people with learning difficulties who live in the district that the team covers and there are the different geographical communities that those individuals with learning difficulties live within. It may well be that there are other communities as well. For instance, one of the authors once knew someone with learning difficulties who was a member of an artistic community, and another person who got a great deal of support from a local martial arts club and from an international virtual community of people who were interested in the same martial art.

Thinking about the potential for people with learning difficulties and their allies, friends and families as a community in the sense of being a network of potential reciprocal relationships could be a useful way of tapping into supportive resources, as well as ways of providing information and assessing the expressed needs of the community. Indeed, many areas of the country already have People First organisations running, and they have proved to be dynamic and supportive communities.

It may prove advantageous to Jenny's team to invest time in making links into this community, perhaps through a collective organisation such as People First. Contact with a local university to set up a student placement to carry out a community profile among other practice learning opportunities could also be extremely helpful to the team, the community and to the student. The social capital (Jordan, 2007) inherent in this community is a huge potential resource to Jenny as she struggles with individuals and families who find themselves in crisis. It is also important for Jenny to understand the sense of community for each individual with whom she works. The community may be supportive in the way suggested above, although we know from a number of unpleasant stories in recent years that local communities can include people with attitudes and behaviour towards people with disabilities that could prove very dangerous (see, for example, BBC News, 2008; Carter, 2010). The team could then start to use their advocacy skills on behalf of the whole community and their expressed needs, rather than just the needs of individuals. The accumulation of data collected from such projects, plus that gleaned from the collation of unmet needs statistics, would start to build a picture that could inform strategic management in planning how resources might be used. If a voluntary or user-led organisation such as People First conducts a campaign around resource cuts, then collective action between them and practitioners as trade unionists could be a very effective approach (Ferguson and Woodward, 2009).

Engagement with voluntary or service user-led organisations would enable a relationship to be built in which a flow of information could help both the represented community and the team. We have noted already the importance of knowledge about community as neighbourhood or reciprocal caring relationships, and, if they are going to be able to signpost people to those supportive resources, community social workers need to engage with these organisations. In return, the team would be able to provide the community and those in need within it with information that was crucial for them to access resources to maintain well-being and quality of life. One aspect of practice that the team need to think about is accessibility or community presence. However, in today's specialised services, teams tend to cover huge geographical patches, a fact that is not conducive to being visible in the community. Jenny's team needs to be imaginative in thinking of the places where their community meets, and ensure that they are regularly available in those places.

Group work is rarely an approach to social work practice that is engaged in contemporary social work organisations. It is, however, an important aspect of community social work in that it enables social workers to engage with several service users' needs at one time, and also because it enables representatives of communities of need, such as people with learning difficulties, to have a voice in the development of services. Jenny and her team, as community social workers and other professionals, could use group work skills to provide collective services to service users, and to facilitate representative community groups to have their say, with information being passed through management to inform decision making.

We would argue that most of the ideas for action listed above for Jenny and her team will be unrealisable unless space is created within the crisis workload of the whole team to start building some of the more preventive services listed. Workload management systems that meet the needs of both managers and professionals are notoriously difficult to develop. One of the problems is that what counts as work is largely determined externally and then relayed to teams, so first line managers need to be proactive in creating space, perhaps through a pilot project, to try out new approaches to practice that may, in the longer term, prove to be effective in preventing crises. There is some evidence of community social work preventing crises (see, for example, Hadley and McGrath, 1984), but social workers and their colleagues need to have their overall workload protected to be able to demonstrate this.

Hasan

We have noted the symptoms that Geoffrey is experiencing from his PTSD that brought him to the attention of Hasan's team. The question is, how might community social work help Hasan and Geoffrey improve Geoffrey's current circumstances and his well-being?

It would appear on the face of it that Geoffrey has lost all contact with any family or community supports that might offer reciprocal caring relationships. This remains no more than an assumption without the active exploration of the community that Geoffrey inhabits and the meaning it has for him, and with the absence of any knowledge of the informal supports available within the community to which he might be linked. It may well be that there is a formal or informal group, perhaps linked to a voluntary organisation such as Mind, that provides just such a community with which Geoffrey could link. There may also be a Zimbabwean community within the town where he is now living which could both understand and provide support to him. Networking into these potential community supports, understanding the meaning of these things to Geoffrey's individual identity, would be a key aspect of social work practice in the community and could make a substantial difference to Geoffrey – possibly more than the medicalised services that are habitually available to mental health service users.

On the negative side, it is important for Hasan to recognise the possibility that Geoffrey is vulnerable within the community where he is living. Oppressive attitudes, often built on ignorant press stories about mental illness and racism in local communities, can cause extreme distress that would add to that already being experienced by Geoffrey. It is in this context that Hasan may want to think of the diversity within communities as consisting of either positive, negative or neutral forces for Geoffrey's well-being. However, unless Hasan and his team build a good knowledge of that community, perhaps through a community profile project, or through making links with voluntary and informal networks, then it is going to be difficult to do more than respond to Geoffrey's crisis needs.

In order to be able to enable Geoffrey to make use of identified formal and informal supportive networks within the community, Hasan needs to use all his skills to ensure his assessment of Geoffrey's needs reflects the service user perspective, as well as ensuring that Geoffrey is motivated to make those links. Doyal and Gough (1991), as we have seen, argue that there are universal needs, most notably the need for personal and critical autonomy. Organisations representing survivors of mental health services such as Shaping Our Lives have noted that both individually and collectively, service users are not given a voice within services that predominantly reflect a medical model of disability. This results in opinions being based more on professional opinion and seldom on the views of service users themselves. As Doyal and Gough note, this is likely to result in an ineffective approach to needs assessment and satisfaction. In Geoffrey's case, Hasan would, from a community perspective, want to ensure that Geoffrey was listened to (autonomy) and provided with information which would enable him to make informed judgements (critical autonomy) about resources available, whether formal or informal.

We can note here the importance of human rights and social justice in Hasan's practice. With mental health survivors the starting point must be the value of social justice informing professional social work practice, and the collective experience of survivors is important in understanding what social justice means to that community. We could also remind Hasan that service users expect social work expertise to include knowledge of local community resources and the skills to link people into those supportive caring networks.

It may well be that the communities surrounding Geoffrey are not well informed about the potential resources available to support them and to assist them in supporting people like Geoffrey. There could then be a role for Hasan, or someone in his team, to carry out some research into the needs and strengths of the community. By supporting an informal group around Geoffrey or a voluntary organisation providing support services, Hasan would be able to provide a more holistic and acceptable system of support for Geoffrey. If there are gaps in services for people experiencing Geoffrey's difficulties, then Hasan has a duty to use evidence gleaned from a community profile to put pressure on his managers to address these needs. If this required a degree of advocacy on Hasan's part, or providing support to Geoffrey or representatives from his supportive community, then this would also fit well with normative community social work practice.

The ways of working described here are not habitually used within statutory mental health or learning difficulties organisations. There is, however, no reason why, with some rejigging of priorities, a community mental health or learning difficulties team should not adopt aspects of this approach to practice in their everyday work. As noted, the Barclay Report (Barclay Committee, 1982) argued strongly that community social work is not a blueprint for action but more a way of thinking about providing supportive services. Given that the overwhelming amount of support for people like Geoffrey is provided within the community, it is essential to build those supportive relationships in order to prevent people like Geoffrey becoming isolated and consequently increasing his chances of being seriously unwell and a concern to the community within which he lives.

Anti-oppressive approaches to community social work

Community social work, as theory and method, reflects anti-oppressive approaches to practice. Taking a community approach is different from taking individualistic approaches, which could potentially perpetuate oppressive experiences for service users by pathologising and personalising their problems. As we have seen in this chapter, the focus of community social work on partnership, involvement, avoiding assumptions about the nature of communities and the individuals who live within them, and ensuring information is shared rather than 'knowledge mystified' (Parsloe, 1983) is all reflective of anti-oppressive approaches to social work.

Anti-oppressive practice is a fundamental aspect of community social work practice, whereby having a community presence, networking, taking participatory approaches and through community profiling (see Chapter Six), the social worker knows who the groups are that make up the community within which she or he works. Identifying sub-groups or individuals who experience oppression within communities and sometimes from communities is an important first step. A community social worker will not merely work with dominant groups who speak loudest but will seek out those who are marginalised and seek to ensure that their voice is heard in assessments of need and the development of resources or ways of working to meet those needs. In these ways, the community social worker should ensure that their practice is inclusive and does not replicate the marginalisation or oppression experienced by groups within the community. A student on placement a while ago was rightly critical of a voluntary organisation that, in wishing to include men who were parents in the services provided, had an advertising campaign which included an offer of a 'bacon sarnie' for any men who attended. The student pointed out that certain religious groups as well as vegetarians would be excluded by such a campaign despite its good intentions.

Dalrymple and Burke (2006) note a number of useful practices that constitute an anti-oppressive approach which are reflected in community social work. Understanding the structural causes of individual problems rather than blaming them on individuals is an important aspect of their anti-oppressive approach. Dalrymple and Burke define empowerment in a number of different ways which are also reflected in community social work practice. Empowerment as listening to ,and taking account of, service user (or in this case community) views is a fundamental anti-oppressive approach to community social work practice, as is ensuring that members of the community are involved in decision making that affects their lives. The participatory approach of community social work is fundamentally geared towards overcoming the barriers that may exist within communities and the organisations with which social workers work to a practice whereby members of those communities gain control over their lives.

We could not add here that community social work, as it was established in the 1970s, was constituted in order to effect radical social change as Dalrymple and Burke suggest anti-oppressive practice should. Such a radical intention was never intended. The implications of the community social work approach are, however, that practice relationships should change from relationships of a more traditional professional power to one that is more collaborative and empowering.

Strengths and limitations

This chapter has highlighted that the consideration of communities should be central in social work practice. Social workers should consider individuals and individual need, yet this should be placed within the individual's community context and the communal need. There are several strengths and limitations to adopting this way of working within the current political and organisational structures.

Potential limitations include the following:

■ Agency focus on the individual (often in crisis). The most difficult hurdle for this way of working is undoubtedly the custom and practice of most social service organisations as they focus on individuals as their objects of concern and, in particular, individuals in crisis. Social services tend to ration resources by the use of eligibility criteria (FACS)[1] which require individuals to be in crisis (critical or substantial need) before they become entitled to a service. We have noted that more recent government rhetoric has emphasised prevention, choice and empowerment as the key approaches to service delivery while at the same time making cuts in resources which have pushed local authorities to push the eligibility thresholds ever higher. Community social work is limited in this context but of course also provides an answer. The focus on prevention, community involvement, networking with informal care providers and community presence all militate against the crisis approach to addressing problems within communities. Community social workers will, however, always have to contend with managers focused on managerial concerns about targets and performance indicators, as well as colleagues from other organisations who do not share the community perspective on problems exhibited by individuals within communities and who prefer to deal with those problems as belonging to individuals rather than acknowledging the structural aspects of them.

- Lack of community work skills among social workers. In this chapter we have noted the skills required for community social workers, yet there is often a lack of such skills within social work teams. We would argue, however, that expertise in such practices as networking, bargaining, interprofessional practice, advocacy, partnership, information sharing and workload management are all endemic skills within social work. The only difference is that they are generally practised within a framework of services focused on individuals not communities. It is our belief that such skills are transferable to the community context.
- Positive focus on communities. Community social work is constrained by its positive focus on communities and, in its original Barclay Report, formed by an insistence that crisis work might still have to be done by specialist workers. Involvement of the community in participatory approaches might be a fundamental aspect of community social work but we have noted, in relation to Geoffrey, for instance, that some members of communities can be marginalised by their communities as well as within them. This is a potential limitation for community social work.

Potential strengths include the following:

- Empowerment-based approach. The empowering approach of community social work, which focuses on facilitating people within communities to be heard and to be involved in decision making, can create virtuous circles in which involvement increases confidence through acquired knowledge and skills, and success begets success.
- Promotes individuals within communities – taking control of their lives. Community social work fits very well with the rhetoric of public policy from recent governments, as noted in Chapter One. Big Society and the transformation agenda, for instance, both focus on empowerment of people in taking control of their lives through involvement, choice and voice. While we have noted the importance of being wary of these policies in their rhetorical form, they do provide an imperative for looking at working more in line with community-oriented, preventive approaches.
- Promotes social justice. The strength of community social work is also reflected in the congruence between nationally and internationally recognised definitions of social work, which emphasise the concepts of empowerment, involvement and a practice built on social justice. Community social work fits with some of the fundamental approaches to social work practice, as outlined in practice guidance for working with

children and families and within community care for adults, as noted in Chapter One.

Summary and conclusion

We noted at the outset of this chapter that community social work is built on an ethical base. Practitioners whose practice is informed by this set of values will find the need to identify and deal with ethical dilemmas. The current system for dealing with people who have serious mental ill health creates huge ethical dilemmas for social workers in much the same way as the organisation of practice in children and adults services. Eligibility criteria that require individuals' and families' support systems to collapse before a service is provided are unethical, let alone uneconomical. It is always the case that people will have crises, both predicted and unforeseen, and social workers, along with colleagues from other professions, will need to be there to help people through them. But when we know that preventive support within people's own identified communities and networks of reciprocal relationships can enable them to work through difficulties before they become crises, it is very damaging for professionals to recognise that they are increasingly part of the problem rather than the solution. Reflecting on the values of social work enables us to note the ways in which a service may stigmatise and exclude individuals, groups or communities. Community social work, as described in this chapter, provides the knowledge, skills and values to promote services that reduce discrimination and promote equality. Community social work is, therefore, a helpful approach for any professional who wants his or her practice to make a difference to the lives of service users and the broader communities in which they live.

Note
[1] Fair Access to Care

Community development

5

Introduction

We now turn to community development, a term that covers a range of different practices. In Chapter Three we looked at a partial history of community development and its links to social work, and this chapter focuses on the practice implications of this approach to social work in the community. Having established some of the areas of practice that are relevant to students or professional social workers, we return to Hasan and Jenny to see how the knowledge, skills and values of community development might assist them in working with service users in their settings.

Community development does, as we say, cover a range of practices, but we only focus on those areas that are of relevance to social workers working in community settings. There are different modes of community development we need to address, some of which reflect a top-down approach to policy implementation (Midgley and Livermore, 2005), as with The World Bank's authoritarian and neoliberal version of community development or the New Labour Action Zone projects of the 1990s, while others are a bottom-up approach, as with the CDPs of the 1970s in the UK, when practitioners took control of the project agenda (Stepney and Popple, 2008). We can also look at community development as seeking consensus between stakeholders in community affairs (Roberts-DeGennaro and Mizrahi, 2005; Ohmer and DeMasi, 2009), or as conflictual, where the community, with professional support, takes on the powerful forces that maintain communities in their state of poverty or marginalisation (Alinsky, 1971; Gilchrist, 2004; Midgley and Livermore, 2005; Reisch, 2005; Mayo, 2009). Community development may be concerned with maintaining the status quo (Motes and Hess, 2007) or transformative (Mayo, 2009; Robson and Spence, 2011), and it can be empowering in its intentions or technocratic.

The clear divide here is between the more consensus or status quo maintenance end of the spectrum and the more transformative or radical end. If we recognise that there are communities that are poor or disadvantaged as a result of the moral choices being made by members of that community, or because of the deficit in their social capital, then the development response is more likely to be focused on changing the individuals and groups within that community. If the approach is built on a belief that the ills of a particular community are the inevitable result of capitalism and the inequality that is created by its social and economic approach (Reisch, 2005), then we need to respond as community development workers by a focus on the oppressive institutions that create and recreate that oppression. If, as social workers, we want to make a difference in the lives of marginalised communities, then we need to be aware that how we see things determines the way we tackle them.

There is discussion in the literature about the concept of power and whether it can be shared or has to be taken, through community development practice. In the consensus model (Ohmer and DeMasi, 2009), it is argued that power is not a zero sum game where, in order for one party to gain power, another has to lose it. Through 'consensus organising' (Ohmer and DeMasi, 2009), practitioners can bring together the marginalised community and the powerful outside agencies in a process in which 'power can be created, shared, and harnessed for the mutual benefit of communities and the external power structure' (Ohmer and DeMasi, 2009, p 13). This partnership and advocacy approach to community development is geared towards community change with 'the deeper and wider the partnership, the greater the capacity for community change' (p 14).

This analysis of power is very different to that of the more radical wing that adopts the zero sum approach. Writers such as Reisch (2005), Gilchrist (2004) and Robson and Spence (2011) argue strongly that an analysis of power relationships is essential practice for community development practitioners. Asking questions such as 'What are we up against?', 'What power have we got?', would be crucial for this approach, as it was for Alinsky's highly conflictual approach to community organising (Alinsky, 1971). Reisch (2005), for instance, argues that community practice should begin with an analysis of 'the root causes of inequality, injustice and oppression, with a particular emphasis on examining the fundamental distribution of resources and power' (Reisch, 2005, p 290). The practice implications of these different approaches are crucial. Does practice set about reaching consensus through networking and relational practice? Does it seek to build links in which power will be shared between communities and organisations that currently hold power? Or does it seek methods for seizing power from those individuals and organisations whom, it is believed, will be unlikely to collaborate in any process that will reduce their power base?

There is also a distinct difference between community development that reflects the beliefs about good communities held by managers, professionals or politicians and is imposed from the top down, through organisational or policy directive, and development practice which facilitates, enables or empowers communities to determine their own destiny. One of the key values of community development is that of community involvement in development processes. All the literature talks of the importance of community involvement, participation or focus as key values for development practice. Even the top-down approaches of New Labour's

Action Zone CDPs were designed to empower communities to make the running in their regeneration. Despite these mutually agreed aims, it has been argued (Gilchrist, 2004) that the externally imposed target systems and performance criteria which were part of New Labour's projects had the effect of undermining community voice by imposing an external agenda. Targets also have the effect of stifling creativity that is the product of 'non-directive' intervention that nurtures 'organic development' (Gilchrist, 2004, p 86). Mayo (2009) argues strongly that community development is a long-term approach to making a difference in community life and it is undermined by the imposition of short-term targets. At the institutional level there is a danger that the natural authoritarianism of institutions requires communities to adapt to the organisation rather than the other way round (Ward, 1973).

While we look at the practice suggested by the consensual approaches mentioned here, we focus more on the practice that seeks to make a difference in marginalised individual and community lives. It is our belief that social work practice is inextricably linked with human rights and social justice (IASSW and IFSW, 2004). The implications of this are that social work must be involved in processes by which relationships are transformed from those that perpetuate oppression and discrimination to ones that reflect equality and social justice. Individuals experience oppression and discrimination, but it is a collective experience (Jordan, 2007) in the sense that oppression labels and stereotypes people and treats them as if they were part of an identified homogeneous group. So any practice that addresses oppression, discrimination or racism must be responsive to this collective experience, and must be transformative in nature. Jordan (2007) also argues that a commitment to equality means understanding inequality and how it is socially structured.

So what might community development that aims to be transformative, or make a difference in the lives of communities, look like in practice?

Community development practice

There are four ways of practising that we want to look at: community empowerment, networking, advocacy and building social capital. There is considerable overlap between these but they do provide us with a good structure for looking at the specific skills of community development. Gilchrist (2004) lists the following seven principles of community empowerment:

1. *Participatory democracy* This, again, is a principle that is common to most approaches to community development. Clarke (2002, p 105) talks about community development as 'the process that puts ordinary

people, as active and valued participants, into planning and delivering [...] changes'. The principle here is the greater the involvement in planning, decision making and evaluation, the 'more beneficial and authentic is the community development method involved' (p 107).

2. *Resources should be as close to the grass roots as possible* This adherence to the principle of localism is, again, common in community development literature, except perhaps when The World Bank is imposing neoliberal strictures such as the privatisation of public assets in developing countries (Midgley and Livermore, 2005).

3. *The starting point for any CDP should be the 'aspirations of the community'* This is the principle of 'voice', which is again widely discussed in the literature (see, for example, Stepney and Popple, 2008; Mayo, 2009; Robson and Spence, 2011). This is where community profiling can be seen as a key part of community development practice (see Chapter Six).

4. *Respecting independence* This represents voice in the sense that it is tempting for professionals, managers and politicians to put their gloss on the issues to be dealt with, but this would undermine the principles of voice and independence.

5. *The management of too much or too little support* This is what Smale et al (1993) refer to as 'marginality'. This is the tricky balance, in practice, between being involved enough to be effective as a facilitator of change, but not so much as to undermine independence or to stifle the voice of the community.

6. *Clarity in relationships* All forms of social work are relational in this sense, and community development is no different. Being clear about the nature of the professional relationship, for instance, between a practitioner and a colleague from a community group, in matters such as responsibility, power and obligation, is essential to effective practice.

7. *Mutuality* The concept of mutuality is a familiar one across the literature. In this case, Gilchrist is focusing on mutual learning. This principle requires all involved in a project to respect and listen to each other's voices in a process of mutual learning in which it is seen that no one person has all the answers to identified problems.

There are other aspects of community empowerment that are key components of community development practice that would make a difference. The process of involvement or participation requires professionals to share power (Goldsworthy, 2002), in some cases handing over power to community representatives. There is a strong argument that such involvement has a therapeutic effect, allowing people to grow as individuals (Goldsworthy, 2002, p 330), to increase their confidence (Gilchrist, 2004, p 44), to validate their humanity and sense of equality (Reisch, 2005), to promote self-help (Midgley, 1986; Robson and Spence, 2011), to offer recognition and respect for diverse cultures (Freire, 1993), and to raise consciousness (Freire, 1993; Robson and Spence, 2011). Saleebey's (2009) strengths perspective is often viewed as being an individualistic approach to social work practice but actually he also used the concept to note the importance of seeing and nurturing strengths within communities.

The second approach to practising is networking, again, widely quoted and discussed in the literature as a key aspect of community development, as we noted it was for community social work in the previous chapter. The Barclay Report referred to the importance of primary (family) and secondary (community) support or caring networks as being the most important and preferable to formal care, and so do Hardcastle (2011). They refer to these levels of support as 'preferable and more conducive to client empowerment than a dependency on tertiary supports and social agencies' (p 295). Like Barclay, they note the preventive possibilities of social workers linking into and nurturing informal networks. Stepney and Popple (2008, p 68) also note the preventive potential when social work practice is informed by good research evidence: 'knowledge of the local community, its networks and resources'.

Two other aspects of networking are making alliances and partnership. Sharkey (2007) argues that networking is a crucial aspect of partnership work, noting that, in health and social care, there is evidence that support networks are crucial factors in positive outcomes for service users, so assessing, analysing and supporting those networks are crucial aspects of effective practice. (Sharkey's discussion of network analysis is too detailed for our purposes here, but would be worth readers following up.) Networking also fits with arguments about social capital that we have explored elsewhere (see, for example, Putnam, 2000). Putnam has demonstrated, quite convincingly, that where there are strong networks and a wide range of voluntary organisations, there is less crime, better health, more wealth and better education. We noted in Chapter two that the cause may actually be in reverse — that financially capitalised neighbourhoods will inevitably do well in social capital as well — but this is not an argument for ignoring the importance, in community development literature, for understanding, strengthening and making use of community networks.

Gilchrist (2004, p 30) conceptualises networks in opposition to organisations, noting that the key aspect of the former is their 'informal connections' as opposed to the bureaucracy inherent in the latter. She notes that networks, being less formal, can maximise trust and reduce power problems, although they can also be prone to avoiding conflict and incompetence. Gilchrist argues the functions of networks can enhance the skills, knowledge, confidence and organisational capacity of communities so that they can better engage with formal decisions made by statutory organisations. A well-developed network can empower a community by this process. The more involved a community is in decision making, the more powerful it becomes. In fact, Gilchrist argues that 'collective action is empowering in its own right' (p 30), when networks assert their interests and influence decision making.

Advocacy is an interesting aspect of community development practice in that it would seem to undermine the notion of self-determination, involvement and participation that are argued as fundamental values for the practice. It is mostly discussed within the consensus models of community development practice; for instance, Hardcastle (2011) suggests four basic skills for advocacy. The first is persuasion, which should be based on facts, knowledge of the power held, being clear about what is wanted and using both emotion and logic in clear, simple language. The second is representation, in which the advocate will clearly take sides and speak up for the community, using effective communication skills within established forums, presenting options that are predetermined by the community themselves, and then sticking together. The third skill is negotiating and bargaining, in which the advocate needs to know what their position is, what they can compromise on and what decision-making powers others in the forum hold, if any. There is no point negotiating with the puppet – you want to see the person who pulls the strings. The fourth skill is bargaining and problem solving, at a micro level, such as using body language or knowing where to sit. One of the authors once observed a community development worker arriving at an important meeting *with* a key power broker in a negotiation that instantly distanced him from the community representatives. It was an unintentional but crucial error. Knowing what the options and alternatives are and the interests of different parties is an essential part of bargaining for problem resolution. There are also other fundamental skills here, as elsewhere in social work practice – of effective communication, building trusting relationships and demonstrating commitment to achieving a solution.

Building social capital is the fourth aspect of community development practice that should be addressed. Hardcastle (2011) argues that building social capital is a central part of overcoming social exclusion and ensuring social justice in community development practice. Gilchrist (2004, p 5) sees social capital in the 'shared expectation', 'reciprocity' and 'mutual obligation' of cooperative practice. Gilchrist's view is that 'the "essence" of community is to be found amongst relationships rather than physical environment' (p 25), and it is through positive networking which builds these relationships that social capital is built. Following Putnam (2000), Ohmer and DeMasi (2009, p 12) distinguish between bonding social capital (the internal capacity of communities) in which locality development will build 'the capacity of community residents to solve problems and foster social integration' (p 12), and bridging social capital, where strong communities can engage in 'creating social networks' (p 12) with a range of external organisations, especially those with resources and decision-making powers.

We now look at some specific skills of community development practice. The more transformative end of the practice spectrum notes the importance of critical reflection as a key skill for practice. Freire (1993) suggested problem posing as a form of critical reflection, in which practitioners, in collaboration with the communities they were engaged with, would look at any proposed development and analyse it by looking at what problems it created, and for whom. Who did the development favour most and were these people already in power, or was it more likely to favour the poor and oppressed? In a similar vein, Goldsworthy (2002, p 334) talks of the development model involving 'continually questioning how we operate and avoiding reactionary practice'. We can link this notion of critical reflection to Doyal and Gough's (1991) theory of universal need, in which they argue that critical autonomy is essential for anyone to be able to achieve satisfaction of their needs. They define autonomy as the ability to have a voice in the decision making over resource development and critical autonomy as the ability and opportunity to be able to make judgements about the purpose of resource development and whom it was going to benefit most. Collaborative, community-based, critical autonomy, we argue, is a central part of effective community development practice.

In discussing the skills of networking in community development, Gilchrist (2004, p 95) interestingly focuses on working on the 'edge of chaos'. She describes community development as inevitably chaotic (perhaps part of Schon's swampy lowlands of community practice; see Schon, 1984), and networking as the best way of dealing with the uncertainties of everyday practice. Many voices and perspectives will enable a good response to such complexity and uncertainty and enable the effective worker, with their community, to make good use of the opportunities inherent in 'the unplanned or unpredictable' (Gilchrist, 2004, p 86). This is in contrast to more technicist approaches that seek to establish certainty of outcomes through the application of evidence-based techniques (Mayo, 2009; Robson and Spence, 2011). Crisis theory (Teater, 2010) teaches us that chaotic moments are very good for learning, if people are open to that. Learning, in as much as it requires letting go of dearly held beliefs, can create chaos for individuals and collectives, but the reverse is also true, particularly when the many and diverse voices of a community are pooled together.

Mayo (2009) makes the distinction made at the outset of this chapter between consensual and transformative approaches to practice, although she prefers to distinguish between them as either 'traditional/technicist' or 'radical/transformational' (Mayo, 2009, p 133). Either way, she argues, there is a whole list of increasingly complex knowledge and skills that community development workers require. These include many of those listed above, as well as assessment skills, participatory action research skills (see Baldwin, 2011, for a discussion of this method in relation to social work practice), group work skills, counselling, management of resources (including of the worker's own time), gaining access to resources (including making grant applications where necessary), recording and report writing and monitoring and evaluation.

We now look at some of the skills involved in practice at the radical end of the spectrum, focusing in particular on Alinsky's (1971) radical community organising (his 'rules for radicals'), feminist community development (see the special edition of the *Community Development Journal*, vol 46, no 3, July 2011) and Reisch's (2005) radical community organising.

It was one of Alinsky's schools for community organising that Barack Obama attended and which educated him as a community organiser before he went into politics. Although these schools of community organising are much less radical these days (Ohmer and DeMasi, 2009), they have a long tradition of producing practitioners who are prepared to take on powerful vested interests, using Alinsky's 'rules for radicals'. We now look at some of these.

Alinsky, as with other radical approaches to community development, was very preoccupied with establishing power relationships. Therefore, one of his rules was 'power is not only what you have but what the enemy thinks you have' (Alinsky, 1971, p 127). Note the use of the word 'enemy'! Alinsky was quite Machiavellian in his use of subterfuge, but it does seem an important principle to be assertive both in your direct work and also in your claims for support from a broad community of interest. There is a wonderful story from the English Civil War in the 17th century when the King's army was at the gates of London at Turnham Green, and the motley array of parliamentarian 'soldiers', mainly consisting of apprentice boys in their livery, turned out to confront them. Also turning out, however, was a substantial proportion of the population of London, who had come to watch the battle. This made the parliamentarian 'army' seem much bigger than it was. The King's army turned around and went back to Oxford, and never tried to attack London again.

'Never go outside the experience of your people' (Alinsky, 1971, p 127) was another rule, and one that reflects what we have said above about the importance of keeping the community's view of needs and issues central to practice focus. Alinsky was also suggesting here the importance of community involvement in campaigns. Their involvement in lobbying, for instance, would do them and the cause a great deal of good.

In suggesting that community organisers should 'make the enemy live up to their own book of rules' (Alinsky, 1971, p 128), Alinsky was suggesting that many organisations had mission statements or were bound to local or national policies to which they might well not be adhering. Pointing this out publicly can be a very powerful tool. 'Ridicule is man's most potent weapon', said Alinsky (1971, p 128), and he cited a number of examples where 'it is not hard' (p 130). He provides the reader with a number of different examples or campaigns that he was involved with in which he, with the community group, identified a key person within the powerful institution and focused attention on them. This is a very radical and controversial tactic but one, from Alinsky's evidence, which works very effectively.

The next section on practice guidance comes from the feminist perspective on community development that rejects the technicist, top-down approaches of projects such as New Labour's Action Zones. Community engagement, argue Robson and Spence (2011, p 291) 'was integral to the understanding of black feminist activists and academics'. This approach has, they argue, informed community development practice in the UK, so that they define feminist community development practice as primarily to do with consciousness raising, which is 'collective, educational and critical' (Robson and Spence, 2011, p 292). The links with Freire's community education approach is made very clear. Robson and Spence also make a distinction between feminist practice and New Labour top-down approaches in the sense that the latter are built on pre-determined policy expectations rather than the 'self-defined and transformative processes' (p 295) that are key to feminist practice. Therefore, providing opportunities for community members to locate 'common experiences of oppression' will build 'relationships and trust between those who share identities in these terms, leading to increased confidence, strength and solidarity' (Robson and Spence, 2011, p 292).

Robson and Spence (2011) are also concerned that the self-help model proposed through the 'Big Society' idea put forward by the Coalition government in the UK means that community development practice will do no more than 'manage and contain the impact of poverty' (p 296). Indeed, the 'Big Society', as well as deep cuts in public services, will 'result in an increased burden of care upon women in poorer communities' (Robson and Spence, 2011, p 296). The use of impact assessments to gauge the degree to which certain groups, for example, women, young people, older people, people with a disability or people from minority ethnic parts of the community, would be a useful way of evaluating this sort of effect. What is more important is to look at specific practices that go beyond identifying problems and to engage with action that makes a difference in the lives of marginalised communities.

This final section is taken from Reisch's (2005) version of radical community development, which is, we must note, heavily influenced by Alinsky and feminist, as well as socialist, perspectives. Reisch starts with three distinguishing characteristics: analysis of 'the root causes of inequality, injustice and oppression, with a particular emphasis on examining the fundamental distribution of resources and power' (p 290). Reisch's radical practice starts from a perspective that capitalism is antithetical to social justice and empowerment, so these relationships of power need to be identified and analysed. As with Alinsky, Reisch argues, in his second point, the need for alternatives to capitalist models of practice as a fundamental distinguishing characteristic. The third characteristic is action to promote 'fundamental structural and institutional change' (Reisch, 2005, p 291).

In terms of approaches to practice, Reisch (2005) has a list of practical possibilities, including feminist empowerment, enabling people to understand their own 'capacities to change their environment' (p 293), and engaging in collective action to confront political power bases. Reisch argues strongly that the community's definition of the problem is always the starting point for analysis and action. He does, however, note the need for Freire-like conscientisation (Freire, 1993) in which communities and practitioners engage in mutually supportive but critical thinking, creating their reality, and de-bunking powerful institutions' versions through critical dialogue. This approach reflects the belief that often individuals and communities will accept status quo thinking until they have the opportunity to think about matters from different perspectives.

Reisch (2005) cites Alinsky a fair deal when it comes to tactics, although he is a little more pragmatic, recognising the need to think about what action is feasible and effective given the wishes and intentions of the community. Not everyone is happy taking direct action, for instance. Reisch also debates whether campaigners ought to use existing political channels or go outside of them using direct action. The problem of the former is the danger of co-optation in which campaigns get sucked into the mainstream, given his maxim that capitalist democracy is 'intrinsically corrupt' (p 296). It is worth remembering Oscar Wilde's quotation here about disobedience: 'Disobedience, in the eyes of anyone who has read history, is man's original virtue. It is through disobedience and rebellion that progress has been made' (Wilde, 1891).

Reisch (2005) provides us with a wonderful list of potential radical community practice which is built on a recognition that a pragmatic approach is essential in a political, economic and social culture such as the US where he is writing, that has no current context of mainstream socialist politics. The lessons for other parts of the developed world such as the UK, but not for places like South America and South Africa, are clear.

- Community development is an educational approach – make the links between 'local issues and their structural causes' (p 298) clear through practice.
- 'Forge connections among groups that have common purposes' (p 298). This is echoed in the UK radical social work literature where social

workers are urged to work in partnership with service user-led groups (see, for example, Baldwin, 2011).

- Adopt creative approaches to involvement and mobilisation, especially with groups such as young or old people who are often marginalised or excluded from organising. Use imaginative approaches to engage people such as the internet or 'the use of cultural activities as vehicles for community development and change' (Reisch, 2005, p 298).
- In order to avoid potential segregation, forge and sustain multiracial and cultural coalitions at local levels, perhaps through outreach work.
- Engage in small-scale community-based action research projects, focused on analysis, learning and solutions. (We talk about community profiling as a form of participatory action research in the following chapter.)
- Build mechanisms of support for practitioners and involved community members – it is tough out there.

Reisch (2005) completes his chapter by providing useful guidance on suitable topics for the education of social workers from a radical perspective. These include talking about class and its effects on working-class communities; noting the effect that work, as constituted under neoliberal economics, has on working-class communities at a local level; making the links between politics and social work clear, especially at the local level; and ensuring that social work students are able to develop skills in community-based action research.

Exercise box 5.1: Community development practice in contemporary social work organisations

Discuss these questions in small groups. Involve colleagues from other agencies, especially service users, if possible.

1. What role might the practices of community development have for contemporary social work?
2. How relevant is the more radical perspective on community development to contemporary social work?
3. How might radical community development practice be introduced as a solution to contemporary social work problems?

Community development in practice

We now return to Hasan and Jenny to see how some of these practical ideas might inform their practice of social work in the community. See pp 41–42 for a reminder.

The individuals that Jenny and her colleagues work with and Hasan's client, Geoffrey, are all, more or less, members of a local community. A good place for Jenny and Hasan to start would be to find out to what degree the voices of the diverse communities that they cover are heard in the strategic plans that their employers use for developing or commissioning services. We have noted the importance of community empowerment with the need for those communities to be involved in decision making. Local partnership boards should be involving community members, although it has been noted, by a group of our students carrying out a community profile for a local People First organisation, that most people with learning difficulties do not know that they have a right to a voice through a partnership board. Getting individuals like Geoffrey or the service users Jenny works with involved in such forums could have an important effect, both collectively and individually. We noted above, for instance, that involvement could have therapeutic effects on individuals and collectively in communities by people learning skills and building confidence.

We look at community profiling in the next chapter, but a project, perhaps a participatory action research project that heard the voices of Jenny and Hasan's communities, could have a powerful effect on the knowledge that their teams use and also on the people involved. A local university may very well be interested in providing a small team of social work students to carry out such a project in collaboration with the community. This is an approach used at several universitites, where social work students engage in community profile projects as part of their first year studies.

Both Hasan and Jenny will already be working in an interprofessional and interorganisational way, ensuring that service users get access to resources from other organisations and professions. What we have noted from this chapter, as in the previous one, is the importance of informal, family and community resources. Unless Hasan and Jenny know what these potential resources are, they will not be able to make links with them themselves or get service users such as Geoffrey involved. This is another area in which community research is essential. Getting service users in touch with informal supports that are happening in pubs, clubs and community halls up and down the country can be an effective way of preventing the kind of emergencies that Jenny and Hasan feel so overwhelmed by.

Using workload management within teams to free up some time for colleagues to engage with the local communities could add to this sense of preventive practice. Hasan or Jenny could, for instance, call a public meeting to give the community the direct opportunity to voice their concerns. Professionals could, if necessary, advise such a meeting of direct action they could take to try and persuade the authorities to listen to these. Such a meeting could target either the general community or the specific part of the community that is experiencing mental ill health or has a learning difficulty. If they do not have the time themselves to do this, Hasan and Jenny could get in touch with voluntary or service user-led organisations working in the area and network support from them for both general and specific difficulties in the community. The nature of support would depend on the needs of the community and the nature of local voluntary organisations. A local Mind group or a service user-led organisation might well have an interest in profiling the needs of the community in order to hear the voices of people attempting to survive the psychiatric system. Representations, through the use of advocacy, could then be made to the statutory services to provide resources to meet those identified needs. Referring service users to these emerging community groups would benefit both the groups and the individuals. As we have seen, the opportunity to be involved, especially when it gives people a sense of purpose and direction, can be therapeutic.

If Hasan or Jenny can create the time and space to be more involved in the development of a community group, be it a geographical or service user community, then they could do well to engage with some of the ideas that Alinsky, feminist community development and Reisch suggest for a more radical practice. It is clearly a difficult position for an employee of a statutory organisation to become involved in the kind of radical action suggested by Alinsky, but there are opportunities here. Consciousness-raising, as suggested by feminist practice, is of great importance for women and for other marginalised individuals and groups, such as mental health service survivors or people with learning difficulties. Sharing stories, discovering common experiences of oppression through self-help or facilitated group work, and then building relationships of trust can lead to increases in confidence, strength and solidarity.

Involvement in such emergent community groups can also give practitioners the opportunity to facilitate, both for themselves and for members of the community, critical reflection or conscientisation, in which all can learn about the connections between local issues and experiences and their structural causes. As Reisch suggests, this enables community groups to learn where to put the pressure for changes in service provision. Social workers do have opportunities to make links with service user groups. We have seen this ourselves, through the links we have made with students, with a range of organisations, representing young carers and people with learning difficulties, for instance at the University of Bath. This again, can be of mutual benefit. Jenny and Hasan could invite representatives from service user organisations to team meetings to discuss their common purposes and to establish the best ways of putting pressure on those parts of organisations that have the power to make important decisions.

In order to pursue this course of action with more marginalised groups such as young people or older people, Hasan and Jenny are going to have to be creative and imaginative. Providing some sort of a hook to hang involvement on is a key approach. Community arts projects can effectively do this, engaging young people who are disaffected in music or dance projects that then enable them to become involved in action to protect the resources within their communities that are important to them.

It would be foolish of us to pretend that any of these ideas are going to be easy for the likes of Jenny or Hasan to put into practice. Many managers within statutory organisations are very focused on the managerial aspects of their role, which are more about securing scarce resources and managing outcomes according to imposed targets, rather than in the more creative aspects of managing professional practice. Where professionals can persuade their managers to create the space for some of this creative work, there is evidence (Stepney and Popple, 2008) that it can prevent crisis referrals. This can only be good for professional practice, team morale and for the well-being of service users and the broader community. People like Jenny and Hasan will, however, need to be well supported by managers who are interested in creative, critical and reflective approaches to supervision and practice development.

Anti-oppressive approaches to community development

Community development, particularly in its transformative expression, reflects anti-oppressive approaches to social work practice (for example, Dalrymple and Burke, 2006). As we have seen, analysis of the causes of inequality and injustice is an important aspect of transformative approaches to community development, as are community involvement, participation, empowerment, collective action and mutual aid.

If we look in more detail at some of these approaches to community development we can see clear links to anti-oppressive social work and the international definitions of social work as an expression of commitment to social justice. Facilitation of change through community members means that the approach is empowering, rather than paternalistic, and this is supported by the quality of mutuality in which respect, listening, and learning leads to collective decision making rather than imposition by powerful members. Another important aspect of this anti-oppressive approach to community development involves the recognition of diverse cultures and perspectives and ensuring that a plurality of voices receives equitable treatment.

Reisch's (2005) argument about identifying power relationships is also a clear indication of an anti-oppressive approach. Indeed his radical approach, in which community development workers are urged to adopt alternatives to capitalist models of practice because capitalist relationships are antithetical to social justice, takes the practice beyond much of what is defined as anti-oppression from an individualist perspective. If the origins of oppression are seen as inherent within structures and institutions, then it is these that must change otherwise practice becomes little more than managing the effects of poverty rather than making a difference in people's lives.

Some of the most helpful anti-oppressive practice implications come from the feminist perspective on community development. Consciousness-raising and facilitating collective action so that communities can confront the power bases that disempower them are practical suggestions for practices. Consciousness-raising is particularly important in relation to the development of critical autonomy, whereby communities need to be aware of the nature of the powerful organisations and individuals with which they are dealing in order for them to collectively stand up to politicians, managers and business leaders.

Strengths and limitations

Potential limitations include the following:

- Agency focus on the individual (often in crisis). Community development does not naturally fit with traditional ways of working within social service organisations, particularly in the sort of statutory agencies that Hasan and Jenny work within. While many practitioners may be attracted to the more radical perspectives of community development, it is going to be very difficult for them, within their roles, to take action that would be in opposition to or questions agency priorities. Workload management to free up time for more preventive approaches may appear to be a sensible approach, but the problem here is that many workload management systems are geared towards meeting managerial targets within current systems rather than a preventive agenda.
- Danger of co-optation. There are limitations when it comes to involving members of the community in consultation. The danger of co-optation is one of these, as mentioned by Reisch (2005). Community leaders can very rapidly lose their commitment to the needs of the community if they get sucked into the mainstream of political practice. This is why the Alinsky maxim of staying close to the community is so important. Much of the more radical end of the practice spectrum involves taking direct action against powerful players. Tactics that split communities and only involve some members can undermine a collective approach.

Potential strengths include the following:

- Empowerment-based approach. Community development that involves community members, is empowering, gives people voice and independence, and facilitates, rather than imposes, change. The community focus which brings with it a preventive perspective is a great strength of community development.
- Supporting networks of relationships and sense of community. Networks of relationships are important to everyone, and help people to deal with difficulties that arise in their lives. Additionally, they are a helpful antidote to the individualism of more mainstream approaches to social work, which tend to pathologise and individualise problems rather than see the structural causes of many of the struggles faced by for people who use social work services.
- Critically reflective approach. The critically reflective approach of community development means it is congruent with social work practice. The suggestion of using Freire's (1996) approach of problem posing in order to identify the winners and losers in any development is also a strength of community development approaches.
- Promotion of 'collective voice'. Last, it is helpful to remind ourselves of Gilchrist's (2004) assertion that many voices and perspectives are essential if you are working in chaotic environments, as social work so often is. Collective voices, from diverse perspectives, coming together through processes of mutual learning and decision-making can build better responses to social troubles than can individual voices, especially if those individual voices are only the most powerful ones and exclude the people who stand to gain or lose from developments.

Summary and conclusion

Community development, particularly in its transformative guise, takes us to the most radical wing of social work in the community. While this might seem to preclude some of its approaches from being pertinent in statutory settings, or even in voluntary sector organisations that are commissioned by health or local authorities, it does suggest practices which are logical within an overall framework of professional social work practice as defined internationally, and, indeed, provides an approach which has some resonance with government policy on empowerment, choice and voice.

The practices suggested in this chapter, which we have listed and analysed in the context of Jenny and Hasan's world of social work, would be difficult to enact but not, we would argue, impossible. What is required is a commitment to the values of social justice, a recognition that it is in communities where people mostly want to receive support and help, and an approach that is facilitative of collective action rather than focused on individual pathology. With support from managers prepared to provide workload management to free up time for such collective and preventive approaches, community development practice could be a useful tool in the locker of the social worker in the community.

Community profiling

6

Introduction

The practice example from Chapter One (see pp 1–2) illustrates a complex situation for Irene as a social worker upholding the importance of diversity, inclusion and anti-oppressive practice yet acknowledging that the services provided to the community are not actually adhering to these values. Irene realises that the operations and delivery of services might actually only meet the needs of a particular subgroup of the community, which overshadows the needs of the community as a whole. She is faced with the task of soliciting the needs of the community as a whole, versus just a few, in order to maximise the services of the Sure Start centre and to truly make the centre a service that meets the needs of the community as defined by the community. A community profile is one approach to social work practice in the community that Irene could use to accomplish this task.

In a general sense, social workers are often employed to work with 'communities of need', or groups of individuals who share a similar situation or common experience (Twelvetrees, 2008). Communities of need could be comprised of people with disabilities, older people, LGBT individuals, individuals with alcohol or drug dependencies, mental health issues or people from minority ethnic backgrounds. Such communities are often defined as 'in need' as they may experience discrimination and/or oppression from the dominant society and may be excluded from access to resources, public or social services or power over themselves and within their communities (Twelvetrees, 2008). The challenge for social workers often lies in determining the actual need of the communities in which they work, particularly as their 'needs' are often defined by government officials, academics, service providers or others who have some sense of power and control over the communities. Social workers, while working to promote social justice, anti-oppressive practice and empowerment, must assess whether individuals and community members have been given the opportunity to define their own needs from their perspectives and experiences and determine whether the identified needs are being adequately addressed.

There are several ways in which social workers can solicit the needs of the community, with each technique involving different levels of community participation. Hawtin and Percy-Smith (2007) have identified four types of activities or techniques that can be used in gathering the needs of communities: (1) needs assessment; (2) community consultation; (3) social audit; and (4) a community profile. Although each of the techniques are similar in that they seek to establish the current needs of the community, identify strengths and resources, and include members of the community in the process, they vary in regard to the actual purpose of the activity, who leads and participates in the activity, and the extent to which the community is consulted, participates, collaborates or leads the activity (Hawtin and Percy-Smith, 2007). A needs assessment tends to analyse and explore existing data (such as secondary data) for a particular purpose with little to no participation from the community members. For example, a social worker may analyse the local GP surgeries' databases for the number of post-partum women who see their GP due to signs of depression to explore the possible need for a post-partum depression women's support group. A community consultation has an aspect of community involvement in that the community is consulted on one or more proposals for action as identified by an agency. A consultation could include the local authority seeking community feedback in regard to the distribution of wheelie bins or rubbish bags in regard to rubbish collection. A social audit involves measuring non-financial activities to determine the overall 'health' of the community. The complete picture of overall 'health' involves analysing the social, economic and environmental benefits and limitations. For example, a local authority may conduct a social audit on a local community to determine whether their diversity promotion programmes have led to reduced racism within the particular area. Finally, a community profile seeks to assess the strengths, resources and needs of a community in collaboration with the community members themselves, such as working with the Local Coalition for Older People to assess how older people view the Meals on Wheels programme.

This chapter covers the concept and activity of a community profile and the use of a profile to define needs as one way of practising social work in a community context. It uses the practice example of Irene and the Sure Start centre to illustrate the type of problem that a social worker or social work team might encounter in understanding the needs of the community in which they work. The chapter begins with a thorough definition of a community profile, a discussion on the relevance of a community profile for effective community-based social work practice, particularly by building on the theories, values and critical concepts as discussed in Chapter Two, an explanation of how to define and select a community to profile, an illustration of the steps of conducting a community profile and a discussion on how to engage communities from an anti-oppressive approach. The chapter ends with examples of communities to encourage readers to think of how they can engage and collaborate with communities in order to assist in defining need.

What is a community profile?

A community profile is one type of activity or technique that can be used to solicit the needs of community members. According to Hawtin and Percy-Smith (2007, p 5), it is defined as follows:

> A *comprehensive* description of the *needs* of a population that is defined, or defines itself, as a *community*, and the *resources* that exist within that community, carried out with the *active involvement of the community itself*, for the purpose of developing an *action plan* or other means of improving the quality of life in the community.

This definition of a community profile has six independent, yet interrelated concepts that contribute to the distinctiveness of this type of activity: comprehensive, needs and resources, community, active involvement of the community and action plan. Each of these is discussed in detail below with needs and resources combined.

Comprehensive A community profile is comprehensive in the sense that it operates from the premise that individual and community needs are not static and are not easily and neatly defined, but are instead a result of interactions between individuals, families, groups and communities and are therefore fluid and multidimensional (Hawtin and Percy-Smith, 2007). In this sense, a community profile can be viewed as being congruent with social systems theory. Social systems theory can best be described by the expression, 'the whole of a system is greater than the sum of its individual parts', and is concerned with assessing the development and transformation of systems (such as individuals, families, groups, communities and society) and the interactions and interdependencies between them (Teater, 2010). This theory emphasises the individual as a system, within her or his community, which is also a system, and assesses and explores the interactions and relationships between the two versus looking at either in isolation. Therefore, a community profile is congruent and embedded within the social systems theory as it encourages social workers and community members to assess the interactions, transactions and relationships between individuals and their environment in order to promote continual positive growth and development (Germain, 1979). A comprehensive community profile seeks to explore these interactions and interdependencies within a community in order to identify and define holistic needs that considers community members within their environment.

Needs and resources A community profile seeks to identify the needs of the community as defined by the community. The identification of needs is not in isolation, but should be explored in relation to existing community strengths and resources. Resources can include material resources (such as food, water, shelter, clothing or transportation), educational and developmental resources, social and emotional support, justice resources or economic resources, such as access to goods and services (Andrews and Motes, 2007). Strengths can include any personal, interpersonal or environmental characteristic or attribute that has the potential to stimulate positive growth and change, such as capacities, assets, capabilities and resources (Saleebey, 2009). Resources can be both tangible and intangible. Considering the social systems theory, the assessment and identification of strengths and resources should be multidimensional by considering individual, familial and communal levels. Through this assessment, the resources of a community may be either under-used, blocked to some or all community members, or are non-existent but could be potential resources (Andrews and Motes, 2007). Identifying the current and potential strengths and resources can assist in identifying and understanding community needs. Although needs tend to focus on the deficits of a community, Hawtin and Percy-Smith (2007) point out that allocation of resources and service provision tend to be based on identified need; therefore, a comprehensive community profile that explores strengths, resources and need is crucial in providing the necessary services to communities and community members.

Community The concept of community is often contested and can be defined in numerous ways, such as in regard to a geographical area, administrative area or a group of individuals with a shared interest or characteristic (see Chapter One). Weil (2005) identifies communities as either geographical or functional. A geographical community can include small villages or large cities, but is defined by visible or established boundaries, whereas functional communities are those that share a specific concern or identity. Both types of communities participate in communication, interaction and an exchange process (Weil, 2005). Such examples of functional communities could include the deaf community, LGBT community, women, parents, a black or minority ethnic group, children, people with mental health needs or individuals in recovery from alcohol and other drug use. Although these definitions are widely accepted, care must be taken in assuming that all individuals of a particular geographical area or with a common interest or characteristic actually feel apart or included within the 'community'. Hence the importance of involving the community in defining the community, determining needs and implementing services where and when appropriate.

Active involvement of the community A community profile seeks to have the active involvement of the community, particularly in defining needs. Weil et al (2010) stress the importance of the active involvement of the community because the community has particular expertise about the strengths and resources that are embedded within it. Additionally, the active involvement of the community promotes empowerment by giving the community a voice, developing skills, techniques and confidence, through participation in the profile process itself, and greater awareness of the strengths, resources and needs of the community.

Action plan A community profile has an end goal of producing an action plan to build on the strengths and resources of the community, seeking to meet the needs as identified by the community. Hawtin and Percy-Smith (2007, p 8) propose an action plan that identifies issues, priorities, actions to be taken and set goals and targets, and proposes a progress monitoring plan.

Irene's use of a community profile

A community profile would be appropriate in addressing Irene's concerns with the Sure Start programme as she has identified that there are services being provided to the community, yet only a subgroup of the community are currently interacting with such services. Irene acknowledged that the Sure Start centre seeks to provide services to the parents, carers and children of an ethnically diverse neighbourhood, yet those who use the centre are predominately white heterosexual women and white children. Irene has identified that a community profile would be a useful tool in determining how to provide services that are in line with the needs of the community as a whole versus a subgroup, and has established an initial aim of 'including a wide range of members from the community to determine the community's needs and subsequently collaborate and participate in programme planning and utilisation of the services at the centre'. Based on the above definition of a community profile, Irene needs to plan for the following actions: (1) participate in a comprehensive needs assessment where she and the community members jointly assess the interactions, transactions and relationships between individuals and their environments in order to define need and meet the overall aim; (2) identify the needs of the community as defined by them while assessing for community strengths and resources; (3) define the community as either those individuals living within a geographical area, administrative area, having a shared interest or characteristic, or a combination of the three; (4) solicit the active involvement of the community members; and (5) create an action plan that specifies the needs, strengths and resources of the community while also setting out strategies and action points to meet the overall aim.

Relevance of a community profile to social work practice

As discussed above, through the five aspects, a community profile can be closely linked to the activities of social work and the theoretical frameworks and values that guide the social work profession, particularly empowerment, the strengths perspective, social constructivism, the theory of human need and social systems theory (see Chapter Two for overviews on each). A community profile is one tool to assist social workers and community members in jointly assessing the strengths, resources, relationships and needs of a community as well as the role that the community plays in meeting the needs of the community members and the needs of the community members that are not being addressed.

As well as being used to identify the needs of communities, a community profile may also be used to meet the needs of social services within or servicing communities. For example, social services in the statutory sector are often encouraged or required to conduct needs assessments of the community members for which they serve or are responsible for serving under legislation (for example, National Health Service and Community Care Act 1990, Children Act 1989, Equality Act 2010 and Disability Discrimination Act 1995). Such needs assessments may seek to determine the percentage of the population that are disabled, from a black or minority ethnic group or require community care services. This exercise usually seeks to determine whether policy priorities are being met and the appropriate allocation of resources. A community profile could replace this type of assessment by involving the community in defining themselves and in determining the type of services that would best suit their needs (Hawtin and Percy-Smith, 2007). This may not only serve a purpose of defining need and services, but could also assist in obtaining information about how services were meeting policy priorities, the processes through which this was taking place and an assessment of the accuracy of allocation of resources based on the correlation between policy priorities and community need (Hawtin and Percy-Smith, 2007; Motes and Hess, 2007; Weil et al, 2010). This exercise and evaluation could lead to changes in programme delivery or policy priorities that more accurately reflected the needs of community members. Community profiling projects could also be carried out by voluntary organisations in an effort to define community needs, to develop services based on community need or to provide recommendations to service provision by statutory social services to more accurately distribute or deliver services.

Exercise box 6.1: Community profiling and social work practice

In pairs or small groups, discuss the following:

1. What are the areas of practice where a community profile would be appropriate?
2. How would you envisage using a community profile in your social work practice?
3. What are the benefits and challenges to using a community profile in social work practice?

Irene as a social worker and the use of a community profile

A community profile is congruent with Irene's role as a social worker as she needs to consider the person-in-environment and conduct an assessment in collaboration with community members on the community's needs, strengths and resources. Irene should promote the interests of community members by seeking their definitions of the community's needs, strengths and resources and by collaborating to implement services that will meet the identified needs in a way that was meaningful and useful to community members. A community profile would enable Irene to use social work theories and methods, such as social systems theory, by conducting an assessment of people in their environments, the strengths perspective and empowerment approach, by assessing and using strengths and resources and collaborating on defining need, identifying, implementing and using services, and social constructivism, by acknowledging communities as variable and each community as the expert versus having all expertise lying with academics, researchers, administrators or policy makers.

Putting a community profile into practice

Before we illustrate the six-stage implementation of a community profile, we first address two main issues that require further explanation and consideration, which include the selection and definition of the community and the level and depth of community member involvement.

Selecting and defining the community

One of the first tasks in conducting a community profile is to select and define the community that is going to be profiled. As stated under the definition of a community profile, the concept of community can be defined in numerous ways, such as those residing in a geographical location or administrative area, or a group of people with a common interest or common characteristics. Willmott (1989) argues that in addition to a common characteristic or interest, a community indicates some level of attachment and interaction among the members of the community. When combining both aspects of common characteristic and attachment and interaction, the meaning of community can be seen as referring 'to those things which people have in common, which bind them together, and give them a sense of belonging to one another' (Day, 2006, p 1), yet this concept of community has been contested as it implies 'as much an aspiration as it is a reality' (Stepney and Popple, 2008, p 7). As can be seen there is not one definitive conceptualisation of community, and therefore the first task within a community profile is determining the definition of community that best fits the aims and objectives of the profile itself.

All three potential ways of defining a community are acceptable within a community profile. Thinking of community in terms of a group of people with some commonality is most likely the simplest starting point. This way of thinking can encompass a commonality of geographical location, such as a single street, neighbourhood, postcode, school district, village, town, city, county or nation, or, alternatively, a group of people who may or may not reside in close proximity to one another but who have a shared characteristic or interest, such as age, gender, ethnicity, nationality, special need, shared problem, political affiliation, occupation, education or religion (Hawtin and Percy-Smith, 2007). A community profile does not have to focus on just one of these areas, but may actually combine one or more, such as pregnant women within a particular school district. Therefore, selecting and defining a community in a community profile involves determining the type of commonality that brings and potentially, yet not necessarily, bonds individuals together to form a community.

Defining the community

Irene needs to begin a community profile by defining the community with which she is going to work. Her definition of community is based on the potential clientele of the Sure Start centre. Therefore, she has defined the community as all parents and carers of children under five years old within the geographical area serviced by the Sure Start centre. In this sense, Irene has defined this community both in regard to a geographical area and as a group of individuals with a common characteristic or interest. Once Irene begins to work with members of the community she will need to verify that this definition of community is accurate and best fits with the aims and objectives of the community profile.

Collaborative approach to determining need

One key aspect that is distinct to a community profile is the active involvement of community members. Hawtin and Percy-Smith (2007) acknowledge that a community profile can be conducted without the involvement of the members of the community, but the risk to this approach is an inaccurate picture of the community and its needs from the perspective of the community members. A community profile is seen as one aspect of community social work and, therefore, by keeping in alignment with the values of social work, a community profile promotes the active involvement of the community members in identifying and building on their strengths and resources and in defining community need, all in an effort to promote growth and positive change. A collaborative approach can lead to an empowered community by acknowledging strengths and resources and developing skills and responsibilities that can promote confidence (Twelvetrees, 2008). Just as working with service users on a micro level, if the community members do not feel that they have a voice in what most affects them, then they are less likely to be involved or to assist in implementing change.

Level and depth of community involvement

There are two issues that should be considered when beginning a community profile and determining the level of involvement of community members (Hawtin and Percy-Smith, 2007). The first involves the level of participation and control and the second is the depth of involvement of community members. Each of these are now discussed in turn.

First, the level of participation and control by community members involves a determination of the extent to which community members consult, participate or control the activities and processes of a community profile. This can be viewed as four points on a continuum, as described by Hanley et al (2004) and McLaughlin (2006), with omission/commission on one end of the continuum followed by consultation, collaboration and then service user/community member control on the opposite end (see Figure 6.1).

Omission/commission involves a public statement of community members' involvement in the community profile, but the actual structure and activities of the profile prohibit or greatly limit the members' actual involvement. Omission refers to a tokenistic approach to community members' involvement, such as seeking the views and perspectives of the members in regard to the profile's aims, objectives or design, but then refusing or failing to implement them into the profile, or simply failing to take the members' needs into consideration when planning the profile,

Figure 6.1: Level of participation and control by community members

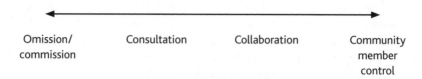

| Omission/ commission | Consultation | Collaboration | Community member control |

such as meeting times and location of meetings (Hanley, 2005; McLaughlin, 2006). Commission, on the other hand, involves the researchers or project leaders predetermining the outcome of the community profile before the profile has actually been conducted. Therefore, any information obtained from the community members is immediately dismissed if not congruent with the predetermined outcomes (McLaughlin, 2006).

The next degree of participation and control is consultation, which involves limited participation in regard to carrying out the activities of the profile itself, but does involve consulting with the community members to solicit their expertise in regard to several aspects of the community profile design or processes. For example, community members may be consulted on how to gain access into a community or consulted on whether they believe the most effective method of data collection should involve focus groups or postal surveys. The process of consultation does not mean that all views and opinions will be followed or implemented, but more likely that they will be taken into consideration when designing and implementing the community profile (Hanley et al, 2004; McLaughlin, 2006).

Collaboration represents a greater level of participation and control and involves joint partnership in the community profile activity. A collaborative approach might involve the community member jointly designing a questionnaire with the researchers or individuals commissioning the project, joint data collection where community members run focus groups or visit homes to gather data, sharing of responsibilities in data analysis and joint report writing. The community members' views and opinions are solicited throughout the duration of the community profiling project and are implemented in subsequent action (Hanley et al, 2004; McLaughlin, 2006). Consultation may occur at any or all stages of the community profiling process, such as the profile design, data collection, data analysis and/or report writing.

Finally, the greatest extent of participation and control is *service user/ community member control*, which requires the community members to control, design and implement the community profile. The power for making decisions lies solely with the community members who are implementing the project, yet the members may seek advice from individuals with expertise in particular areas, such as questionnaire design, data collection or data analysis, or may commission individuals to carry out these specific aspects of the profile. The main criteria involved in this approach is that the power and control lies with the community members who are ultimately responsible for decision making (Hanley et al, 2004; McLaughlin, 2006).

Each of the points on the continuum represents different strengths to which the community members are involved in the community profile. Consultation, collaboration and service user/community member-led are each congruent with social work values to varying degrees such as partnership working, promoting autonomy, empowerment and self-determination, and anti-oppressive practice by soliciting the views, perspectives and gaining the problem, need and goal definitions from the members. An assessment of the strengths and resources of the community can assist in determining which approach to take with the community profile, as the more involved, motivated and skilled a community, the more the profile can take an approach that is closer to the service user/community member point on the continuum.

Second, the depth of involvement of community members can be conceptualised as either a bottom–up or top–down exercise. A bottom–up exercise involves the community members at the ground level taking charge of the community profiling activities and processes and a top–down exercise involves the profiling activities and processes being performed by outside individuals or professionals with consultation from community leaders or members (Hawtin and Percy-Smith, 2007). Although these two approaches appear to be dichotomous, they are actually to be viewed as a continuum, just as the level of control and participation by community members' continuum, where the extent to which community members are active, involved or consulted, is variable. An analysis of the skills, expertise and knowledge needed to complete the profile will assist in determining which approach is most appropriate in reaching the aims and objectives of the profile.

Just as social work practice with individuals promotes a collaborative approach, community social work and community profiling projects equally promote a collaborative approach to defining need. This collaborative approach involves community members defining problems and needs from their perspective, determining goals to meet the identified needs and establishing tasks to reach the goals. Community members are encouraged to take responsibility in achieving the established goals while using their strengths and resources in this process with a potential resource including the skills and expertise of the social workers or researchers who are working with and providing services to the community. The collaborative approach should stretch across all stages of the community profile, starting with the initial design followed by fieldwork and data collection, data analysis and the report writing and follow-up, although this may occur in varying degrees.

Each stage of the process should be designed to encourage discussion with community members and/or key stakeholders to encourage ideas about how best to achieve the aims and objectives, with clear lines for communication between all parties involved (Hawtin and Percy-Smith, 2007).

Additionally, Twelvetrees (2008, p 45) identified a nine-stage tool to help implement a collaborative approach to defining need. The stages are viewed as supporting a collaborative relationship between social workers or researchers and community members that promotes autonomy. Although described as stages, they do not necessarily occur in sequential order, but may take a more non-linear approach. The nine stages are as follows:

1. Contact community members and identify general needs.
2. Bring community members together, help them identify specific needs and assist them to develop the will to see that those needs are met.
3. Help them understand what will have to be done if those needs are to be met.
4. Help them identify objectives.
5. Help them form and maintain an organisation suitable for meeting those objectives.
6. Help them identify and acquire resources (knowledge, skills, money, people, equipment).
7. Help them evaluate alternative lines of approaches, choose priorities and design a plan of action, thus turning strategic objectives into a series of smaller objectives and tasks.
8. Help them divide these tasks between them and carry them out.
9. Help the members of the group feed back the results of their actions to the whole community that then has to evaluate those actions and adopt modified objectives.

We propose that the nine-stage tool could be used in combination with the stages of a community profile (see below) to analyse and reflect the degree to which community members are involved with the project and to ensure a collaborative approach and promotion of autonomy.

Determining level of participation and control by community members

Irene has identified her community and now needs to determine the level of control and participation of community members. Based on her social work values, she has decided to initially start with a collaborative approach where she will work in joint partnership with community members in designing, implementing, analysing and writing up the community profile project. Irene believes that a collaborative approach is consistent with social work values of promoting self-determination, autonomy, the interests of community members, acknowledging community members as experts and giving them a voice through the whole process of the profile. The depth of involvement of the community members in each of these steps needs to be determined after Irene and the community members have conducted an assessment of the skills and knowledge that the members hold in each area. If the skills and knowledge are present among the members, than a bottom-up approach will be appropriate, but if certain skills and knowledge are limited, then Irene and the members will have to solicit outside expertise to collaborate on these activities (such as collecting and/or analysing data and writing up the profile report).

Community profile design

After careful consideration in defining the community and determining the level and depth of involvement from community members, the steps of the community profile project can begin. As discussed above, a community profile is a detailed project that begins with a definition of the community as well as a picture of the community in terms of demographics, characteristics, strengths and resources, which should be determined and collected in collaboration with community members. The aim of a community profile is to explore and identify community needs, as defined by the community, and to develop and implement an action plan for how to address and meet such needs while using and building on its strengths and resources. Hawtin and Percy-Smith (2007, p 24) identified six stages to the community profile process that are discussed in detail here and applied to Irene's community profile.

Preparing the ground

This first stage involves soliciting the involvement of community members, identifying and defining the community, establishing connections with key stakeholders, exploring strengths and resources, identifying outside help and developing a management structure. Each step, as outlined by Hawtin and Percy-Smith (2007, pp 23-33), is further detailed as follows:

1. *Creating a steering group* This first step involves soliciting the involvement of individuals (for example, community members, professionals or other interested individuals) who will act as the steering group for the initial stages of the project and potentially beyond. In some cases active community members may already be identified and involved, yet in

other situations, community members may need to be approached and asked to take part. Careful consideration should be made at this stage to solicit a diverse group of individuals that represents the composition of the actual community in order to prevent the promotion of views of a select few while avoiding or ignoring the views of others. Therefore, recruitment efforts and plans should be well thought out to ensure that all community members and interested individuals are given an opportunity to participate. For example, an agency or organisation could hold a public meeting which details the rationale for a community profile and the need for community members and other interested individuals to assist and contribute to the project, distribute a postal mailing to all community members and other interested individuals requesting assistance or conduct door-to-door knocking to reach those who are usually not engaged with the agency or organisation. Hawtin and Percy-Smith (2007) specify that the size of the initial steering group will vary depending on the size of the community, the aims of the project, the amount of work to be achieved, the time availability and commitment of the group members to the project, and could be as small as two to three people or as large as 12 to 13 (Hawtin and Percy-Smith, 2007, p 25). For example, in creating a steering group, Irene recruited the assistance of two mothers from a mother and toddler playgroup at the Sure Start centre. Together, Irene and the two mothers decided that in order to have a steering group representative of the community they would hold an information meeting at the centre on three different days at different times. The open invitation to the information meetings was displayed in poster format at the centre, at the local shops in the community and on notice boards at GP surgeries and social services agencies. The information meetings described the identified need for a community profile, and the request for volunteers to serve on the steering group. Additionally, Irene identified that a representative from the local authority should sit on the steering group, particularly someone who had input and control over the funding of social programmes within the community, as well as a representative from the local Racial Equality Council who could assist in representing and soliciting the views and involvement of under-represented community members. From the information meetings, Irene and the two mothers recruited an additional five volunteers, making a total of eight members on the steering group.

2. *Initial planning* Once a steering group has been formed of community members, professionals and/or other interested individuals who are able and willing to assist or contribute to the community profile, the initial planning of the profile can take place, which should begin with an agreed definition of the 'community' to be profiled. As discussed in

Chapter One, a community can be defined as either those individuals who reside in a particular geographical area or administrative area or a group of individuals who share a similar interest or characteristic. Regardless of the type of community definition, the steering group must establish a boundary to this definition. For example, if a geographical or administrative area is used, then the actual street boundaries should be identified, or if a group of individuals with a similar interest or characteristic is used, such as women experiencing post-partum depression, then a boundary of age of the woman and age of the child(ren) may need to be established in order to keep the profile manageable (Hawtin and Percy-Smith, 2007). This step also involves exploring the initial aims or objectives of the profile, which are likely to include the initial issues that need to be addressed. For example, Irene defined the community as all parents and carers of children under five years old within the geographical area serviced by the Sure Start centre. The steering group agreed and approved this definition and established the actual street boundaries of the geographical area. The steering group also approved Irene's initial aim of 'including a wide range of members from the community to determine the community's needs and subsequently collaborate and participate in programme planning and utilisation of the services at the centre'.

3. *Making contacts* This stage involves making contact with other members of the community as well as other key stakeholders who may have information about the community, who provide services or support to the community or who represent the community. The contact should include providing information on the scope and aims of the profile, an invitation to be involved by either providing information or supporting the steering group and providing contact details of the steering group in order for the individuals to make contact at their leisure. This contact is usually initiated through a letter with a suggestion that a telephone call will follow to arrange a meeting to discuss, or detailing a focus group or public forum to provide further information. It is important to make contact not only with the community members but also other key stakeholders who may have vital information about the community's needs or who may have the power or resources to meet identified needs in the future. For example, Irene and the other members of the steering group identified that a key stakeholder from the local authority who has power and can make decisions in regard to social programmes in the community should be formally invited to sit on the steering group. Additionally, due to the lack of involvement of black and minority ethnic groups, fathers and homosexual parents and carers with the centre, Irene and the steering group members decided to formally invite a representative from the local Racial Equality Council

to serve on the steering group and to provide recommendations for representatives from these under-represented groups to serve. The invitations to these particular two key stakeholders were presented to the individuals through a formal letter stating the initial aim of the community profile, the need for the individual's representation and the names of the current steering group members. The letter requested a follow-up contact via telephone or in person to formally make arrangements for membership on the steering group. The representative from the Racial Equality Council was able to suggest two individuals from the community who were from the under-represented groups. A total of 12 individuals representing the community and key stakeholders comprised the steering group.

4. *Learning from others' experience and identifying strengths and resources* This step involves exploring the experiences of others who have conducted a community profile or similar needs assessment with the same community or another community. By talking with others, the steering group can learn and model the creativity and skills of others as well as learn from others' mistakes and strategies to overcome obstacles. Additionally, the steering group should conduct an assessment of the current strengths and resources of the community as a whole as well as the skills and resources of the steering group members, which will assist in determining which parts of the project can be conducted from within and which will need to be outsourced to more skilled individuals. For example, Irene made contact with the other Sure Start and children's centres in the area to gather their experiences in gaining and subsequently meeting the needs of the community members, and invited experienced individuals to come and discuss the process of a community profile to the steering group. Additionally, the strengths and resources of the community and the steering group were solicited. The community was examined in terms of resources, such as use of space, money and services, and the steering group members participated in an exercise whereby all members listed their strengths in regard to data collection (individual interviews, focus groups, questionnaire design and implementation, access and understanding of national and local statistics) data analysis (analysis of statistics, transcribing of audio-taped individual interviews or focus groups, collation and analysis of transcriptions), project management skills and report writing skills. This information was recorded and will be used when planning for the data collection and analysis, managing the community profile process and writing the final report.

5. *Engaging consultants or professional researchers* Based on the assessment of strengths and resources of the community and steering group members, external consultants or researchers may need to be approached to carry

out tasks that require specific skills not possessed by the community. For example, on the strengths and resources exercise by the steering group, Irene and the steering group acknowledged that an external consultant should be used to assist in questionnaire design, data collection and analysis. A local university researcher who specialises in community research was approached and asked to provide assistance with the community profile in regard to data collection and analysis.

6. *Development of a management structure* Last, the steering group should devise a plan that details the management structure of the project. This could involve the steering group remaining responsible for the identification of action points, overseeing activities and problem solving or soliciting of members of the community to take on these responsibilities. If the latter is the case, then this person or persons should be appointed in a democratic manner, with the roles and responsibilities being made explicit to both the nominated individual(s) as well as all community members. Additionally, the logistics of running and managing the group should be considered such as the timing and accessibility of meetings, location and any other work or childcare responsibilities that might have an impact on the work and size of the group. For example, Irene and the steering group decided that the group was currently representative of the community as a whole and all were in agreement to carry on the oversight and planning of the community profile. The group acknowledged that new members might be solicited, particularly if they represented the views of individuals currently not on the group. Additionally, the group nominated and elected Irene to chair the group, to take responsibility for organising the meetings and to keep all informed of the process of the project. Other members volunteered to take turns keeping the minutes of the meetings and all agreed to distribute the work according to the skills and availability of the members.

Setting aims and objectives

The second stage involves specifying the aims and objectives of the project in specific and measurable terms. As Hawtin and Percy-Smith (2007, p 33) clarify, 'in most cases the profile will not be an end in itself but a means to an end'. The aims and objectives should be determined and agreed by the whole management group (Hawtin and Percy-Smith, 2007). For example, Irene and the steering group established the overall aim and have determined that in meeting this aim, they would need to achieve the following objectives: (1) determine the demographics and characteristics of the community in regard to ethnicity, parenting type, and other areas; (2) ask a representative sample of the community as to whether and how they currently use the centre; (3) solicit the views and opinions from a representative sample of the community as to what they would like to see provided by the centre; and (4) solicit the views and opinions from a representative sample of the community as to what would make the centre more accessible to them.

1. *Deciding on methods* Once the aims and objectives have been established and agreed, the group can then determine which methods are most appropriate in reaching the aims and objectives. Each objective should be looked at in turn with consideration as to whether information already exists in regard to that specific objective, such as statistics on the community or relevant collation of views of the community, or if the information needs to be collected from primary or secondary sources, such as questionnaires distributed to community members or individual interviews soliciting views or from an analysis of existing data already held on the community. For example, in regard to Irene's four objectives, the following methods were determined necessary to meet each objective: (1) use of existing data to gain a picture of the community, such as census data; (2) use of quantitative methods through closed questions on a self-administered questionnaire; (3) use of qualitative methods through open-ended questions on a self-administered questionnaire; and (4) use of qualitative methods through open-ended questions on a self-administered questionnaire.

2. *Fieldwork* This stage involves the actual implementation of the second and third stages where the methods deemed necessary are carried out. This is considered the data collection stage. Once all the data are collected, they must then be analysed to make sense of the data and begin to answer the original research question or reach the overall aim of the project.

3. *Reporting* This stage takes place after the completion of data collection and analysis (that is, fieldwork), where the findings are written in a report that answers the original research question or aims and sets out action steps to take the findings forward.

4. *Action* This is the final stage where the action points identified from the findings are specified and reported to the appropriate individuals, groups, agencies and/or organisations. Hawtin and Percy-Smith (2007, p 50) clarify that the action points are 'likely to affect the community in some way, perhaps through campaigning for additional resources or changes in service provision, or merely to enlighten and raise the awareness of members of the community and decision makers about issues relevant to that community'.

Anti-oppressive approaches to community profiling

Anti-oppressive practice is particularly important in a community profile as the profile seeks to identify the strengths and resources of a community and to have the community identify their needs that will help them grow and develop. Despite this attempt, there must be an acknowledgement that even within communities where individuals share some common characteristics or need, there are subgroups of the community who may be oppressed. Communities may not always be cohesive or together, and an anti-oppressive approach to the community profile attempts to encourage all community members to express their views. A complete description and definition of the community will assist in determining any subgroups that are currently oppressed and/or not encouraged to participate in community decision making. Failure to acknowledge these individuals or groups and failure to solicit their views and to provide opportunities to participate will only provide an incomplete community profile that continues to promote the views of the dominant group while simultaneously suppressing others.

Hawtin et al (1994) recommend several strategies in moving an oppressed subgroup of the community into an active, more egalitarian position where they are able to express their views and participate in decision making. Such strategies may involve the following: (1) encouraging and motivating the groups to come together; (2) acknowledging and understanding the nature of the oppression being experienced; (3) identifying their requirements for participating and having their voices be heard; (4) developing an action plan; and subsequently (5) taking part in developing services and resources to the community (Hawtin et al, 1994, p 35). This anti-oppressive approach seeks to eliminate barriers that prohibit the active involvement of some community members while motivating and encouraging them to take action in breaking down the barriers and jointly working together to assist the members to have a voice that will be respected and considered. This will ultimately lead to better resources in the community to address need and promote growth and positive change.

Community profiling and anti-oppressive practice

Irene values and implements anti-oppressive practice in her work at the Sure Start centre that led to the initial realisation that the centre's services were only being used by a select subgroup of the community. Irene acknowledged that the uptake of services did not seem to mirror the composition of community members. Irene initiated the process of a community profile in order to work collaboratively with members of the community to identify

▶

the needs that would represent the community as a whole and to encourage all members to use the centre. In this process, Irene acknowledged that she would need to ensure that particular subgroups were not oppressed and was therefore seeking the involvement of members who represent other subgroups either through active involvement in the community profile process or simply by ensuring that their views were solicited and heard. Irene also needs to acknowledge any differences between herself and the community members and be cognisant to how these differences may affect the collaborative work. Irene will start this process by acknowledging the community members as experts in their needs, acknowledging the existing strengths and resources, and realising and respecting that the community's needs, values, norms and wishes may be different from her own.

Strengths and limitations

A community profile has been described in this chapter as an approach to social work in the community that actually involves the community in identifying needs and ways in which to address them. As with any intervention, there are several strengths and limitations when being incorporated into social work practice that should be acknowledged.

Potential limitations include the following:

- *Resources* Social workers working within the voluntary and statutory sectors may be constrained by the time and resources required to conduct a thorough community profile. Social workers are often constrained by the amount of time they are able to work directly with service users and would need additional time and money in order to use this approach. Additionally, managerial support is required, yet with agencies, particularly statutory settings, being constrained by budget restrictions, eligibility criteria and individual assessments, the focus on the community may not be a priority and, subsequently, resources are not usually signposted for community-based work.
- *Expertise in the method* As this chapter has illustrated, the community profiling approach is very detailed and requires expertise in a number of areas, such as knowledge of the community, organisation, research and presentation skills. A social worker would need to become familiar with this approach and be willing and able to develop the necessary skills, which can often require time, money and commitment.
- *Involvement of members* The community profiling approach encourages the active involvement of all community members, yet a limitation to this approach can be that some members may still be oppressed or, due to being a minority, may not have their voices heard. A thorough community

profile will attempt to hear the voices of all community members, yet the reality is that members cannot be forced to participate and the general consensus of decisions, such as the definition of a community, the identified need and the action plan to address the need, will consist of the general consensus. Social workers need to acknowledge this potential limitation and strive to hear the voices of all individuals and reach a consensus that resonates with all community members.

■ *Structural constraints to the community profile* The community profile approach seeks to implement an action plan to solve a problem or meet a need as identified by the community. Once an action plan has been identified, the social worker then needs to ensure that the proposed changes are acknowledged and upheld by structural forces, such as the community, local authorities, agencies and potentially a policy. It cannot be assumed that a community profile will always lead to structural changes and a lack of change makes a mockery of the profile. A recent group of social work students were appalled at the outcome of their profile with a local community when they were informed that the agency was going to use their report as a doorstop. Social workers should be aware of the constraints and limitations to having a profile acknowledged and the findings upheld and put into place strategic efforts to avoid or limit such situations from occurring.

Potential strengths include the following:

■ *Empowerment of community members* A community profile is empowering in nature by soliciting the active involvement of all members, allowing them to be the experts in regard to defining community and need and steering the direction of the action plan. The profile encourages members to be active within their communities and to build a community that would enable the members to have choice and control within an environment that fosters positive growth and development.

■ *Alignment with social work codes of practice and values* The community profiling approach is congruent with the social work codes of practice and values. It promotes the involvement, interests and independence of community members and self-determination and respects the views, wishes and needs of each individual and the community as a whole. This is particularly evident through the practice of working 'with' the community, not 'on' them, encouraging the community to define themselves and their needs versus assuming an outsider (such as researchers, politicians or helping professionals) holds this knowledge, and encouraging the community to be involved in every step of the process in order to promote autonomy and an empowering environment.

■ *Anti-oppressive in nature* A community profile is anti-oppressive in nature by encouraging the community members to become involved in the profile, from defining need to implementing the action plan. A true profile acknowledges that some community members may still be oppressed through this process and will seek to solicit the views of such members and encourage their involvement in the process. A profile will also acknowledge the structural constraints that may limit the effect of the profile and will seek to implement strategies to combat or limit the effects of such constraints.

■ *Holistic in nature* A community profile is influenced by social systems theory in that it seeks to look holistically at the person-in-environment versus taking an individualistic approach. A profile considers how individuals interact and are affected by communities, and how communities interact and are affected by society. Taking an holistic perspective allows for a profile to consider the person in his/her environment and takes the blame away from the individual, placing it into a more structural perspective.

Summary and conclusion

Social workers are often employed to work with 'communities of need' or individuals who share a similar situation or circumstance (Twelvetrees, 2008), yet the 'need' is often defined by others outside of the community, such as academics, administrators or political officials. A community profile is a tool that can be used in social work practice to better understand the needs, strengths and resources of a community while being comprehensive in that it is built on social systems theory, which acknowledges that people interact, affect and are affected by their environments. Not only does a community profile seek to identify need, as defined by the community members, but it also assesses and builds on a community's strengths and resources. A community profile is relevant to social work practice in that it adheres to the social systems theory, as well as the strengths perspective, empowerment approach and social constructivism, where there is an assessment, acknowledgement and utilisation of strengths and resources, the profile is delivered in collaboration with the community members and members are viewed as the experts in their community. These aspects of a community profile contribute to anti-oppressive practice, particularly when the views of those who are marginalised are solicited and represented.

Exercise box 6.2: Applying the community profiling process to three case examples

The following three scenarios depict either a research question or an unexplored topic as presented by an agency, organisation or local authority that provides services to the community. Read each scenario and consider how a community profile might be useful in answering the research question or providing information on the unexplored topic. Discuss how the community could be defined, the level of participation and control by community members that would be appropriate, and how anti-oppressive practice could be used.

1. A local council has noticed a drastic decrease in the uptake of respite care services for older people over the past three months. Nearly three months ago the local council changed the contract of respite care services from being delivered by Agency A to Agency B. The council is curious as to the rationale for a decrease in services and would like to determine if this decrease is due to the change in service providers.

2. A charitable organisation has recently been given a lump sum of money to be used to open a community centre in Town A. The organisation has numerous centres already established across the UK which are widely used by community members who continually positively evaluate the centre. The organisation is beginning the planning stages of the design, purpose and services delivered by this particular community centre and they wonder whether they should model the centre after one of their already established centres or experiment with a new design and purpose.

3. A foster care agency has had a recent decline in the number of registered foster carers, yet the number of children in need receiving services from the agency continues to rise. The agency would like to recruit more foster carers but is unsure about where and how to approach potential carers, and what type of information to provide.

7

Social work in the community: global perspectives

Introduction

As discussed in previous chapters, the concept of community can be defined in several ways, such as, in regard to an administrative area or a group of individuals with a shared interest or characteristic. A community can be perceived as a geographical area, with visible and established boundaries, such as villages or large cities, or as functional communities, such as those that share a specific concern or identity (Weil, 2005). Both geographical and functional communities participate in communication, interaction and exchange information and resources through an exchange process. Often communities are visualised as our proximally close neighbours, our close networks of friends and colleagues, or the group of individuals that share a common interest or characteristics, all of which are relatively small in nature and easily accessible. What is missing from this perspective of community is the fact that communities can actually exist along a continuum, from local to global (Gamble and Weil, 2010). Individuals can identify with their local neighbours, such as those who reside on the same housing estate, with a national group that share a common interest, such as the British Association of Social Workers (BASW), and even with international groups that act as a community in order to address global issues, such as the Fair Trade Organization or human rights organisations.

This chapter explores the concept of global community by describing the social work theories and methods that support this way of working as well as the concepts of social justice and globalisation. It then turns to two related types of global community work practice that occur at the global level – sustainable development and progressive change – and concludes with the global role of civil society and non-governmental organisations.

Global communities and social work practice

The perspective of a continuum of local to global communities represents a progressive view that individuals should not only view their neighbours or those with whom they identify on a personal level as 'community', but rather, should gradually broaden the proximal or functional view of community to a global level. Therefore, communities extend beyond the group of individuals who reside on Main Street in Town A and extend beyond the collection of social workers who work within the UK and are collectively belonging to BASW. Communities can be global to include the social workers, civil society organisations (CSOs) and non-governmental organisations (NGOs) that work across the globe and are joined by the IFSW, or those NGOs that subscribe to the Earth Charter that aims to eliminate the exploitation of people and resources. The basic premises of social work in the community equally apply on a global or international level, and global or international work easily resides with the prominent social work theories and methods that relate to social work and the underpinning values and ethics.

The purpose and aim of social work, as defined by the IFSW and IASSW, is to promote social justice and to enhance well-being, and to intervene at the point where individuals interact with their environment. The IFSW and IASSW (2004) have established an international definition of social work, which states that:

> The social work profession promotes social change, problem solving in human relationships and empowerment and liberation of people to enhance well-being. Utilising theories of human behaviour and social systems, social work intervenes at the points where people interact with their environments. Principles of human rights and social justice are fundamental to social work.

The 'environment', as mentioned in this definition, not only means the immediate relational surroundings of an individual, such as his or her family, friends or local support networks, but can also include the physical and built environment, such as the land or water resources that are necessary in order for individuals to live, thrive and maintain relationships. Working to strengthen the relationship between individuals and their environment may need to occur on an individual level, such as working with a service user to cope with daily stressors in order to maintain employment, but enhancing social functioning may also need to occur on a community level, such as organising a community volunteer rubbish collection day to improve the physical appearance of the local community. Additionally, enhancing social functioning may also need to occur on a global level where issues that are affecting the global community, such as a decrease in the availability of environmental resources, pollution caused by humankind or the spread of disease, requires the attention of the global community and a global community response.

Table 7.1: Eight Millennium Development Goals with 2015 targets

Goals	Target for 2015
1. Eradicate extreme poverty and hunger	Halve, between 1990 and 2015, the proportion of people whose income is less than US$1 a day, achieve full and productive employment and decent work for all (including women and young people), and halve the proportion of people who suffer from hunger
2. Achieve universal primary education	Ensure that, by 2015, children everywhere, boys and girls alike, will be able to complete a full course of primary schooling
3. Promote gender equality and empower	Eliminate gender disparity in primary and women secondary education, preferably by 2005, and in all levels of education no later than 2015
4. Reduce child mortality	Reduce by two thirds, between 1990 and 2015, the under-five mortality rate
5. Improve maternal health	Reduce by three quarters, between 1990 and 2015, the maternal mortality ratio, and achieve universal access to reproductive health
6. Combat HIV/AIDS, malaria and other major diseases	Have halted by 2015 and begun to reverse the spread of HIV/AIDS, and achieve, by 2010, universal access to treatment for HIV/AIDS for all those that need it. Have halted by 2015 and begun to reverse the incidence of malaria and other major diseases
7. Ensure environmental sustainability	Integrate the principles of sustainable development into country policies and programmes and reverse the loss of environmental resources. Reduce biodiversity loss, achieving, by 2010, a significant reduction in the rate of loss. Halve, by 2015, the proportion of the population without sustainable access to safe drinking water and basic sanitation. By 2020, achieve a significant improvement in the lives of at least 100 million slum dwellers
8. Develop a global partnership for	Address the special needs of the least developed countries, landlocked countries and small island developing states. Develop further an open, rule-based, predictable, non-discriminatory trading and financial system. Deal comprehensively with developing countries' debt. In cooperation with the private sector, make available the benefits of new technologies, especially information and communication

Source: UN (2011)

Table 7.2: Top 15 nations as measured by the HDI

HDI rank	Country	HDI value
1	Norway	0.938
2	Australia	0.937
3	New Zealand	0.907
4	United States	0.902
5	Ireland	0.895
6	Liechtenstein	0.891
7	Netherlands	0.890
8	Canada	0.888
9	Sweden	0.885
10	Germany	0.885
11	Japan	0.884
12	Korea, Republic of	0.877
13	Switzerland	0.874
14	France	0.872
15	Israel	0.872
...		
26	United Kingdom	0.849

Source: UNDP (2010)

This striving for an improvement in the social functioning of service users, whether they are defined as individuals, families or communities (local to global), is the mission of social work practice as supported by the prominent social work theories of social systems theory (Buckley, 1967; Specht and Vickery, 1977), person–in–environment (Karls and Wandrei, 1994; Saleeby, 2001) and the ecological perspective (Gitterman and Germain, 2008). According to Bisman (1994, p 27), the person–in–environment is not the simple dual relationship as the theory's title suggests, but rather has three components that consider, 'individuals within the context of the community and its resources, societal policies and regulations and the service delivery of organisations'. Again, communities, whether viewed as local or global, have resources, societal policies and regulations and organisations that provide, to some extent, the delivery of services. This perspective provides a social context to consider when aiming to enhance the social functioning of individuals, families and communities, and to intervene where individuals and families interact with their environments.

Social justice

The aim of social work includes enhancing the social functioning of service users, yet equally strives to promote and sustain social justice. Social work associations across the globe, including the National Association of Social Workers in the US, BASW, the Canadian Association of Social Workers, the Russian Association of Social Workers and the IFSW all affirm a commitment for social justice (Hardcastle, 2011). IFSW (2005, para 4.2) specifically state, 'social workers have a responsibility to promote social justice, in relation to society generally, and in relation to the people with whom they work'. This promotion of social justice spans across all levels of working, from individual therapeutic work to global social change. IFSW (2005) state that social workers have a responsibility to promote social justice, which includes the following:

1. Challenge negative discrimination that is based on characteristics such as ability, age, culture, gender or sex, marital status, socioeconomic status, political opinions, skin colour, racial or other physical characteristics, sexual orientation or spiritual beliefs.
2. Recognise diversity – recognise and respect the ethnic and cultural diversity of the societies in which they practise, taking account of individual, family, group and community differences.
3. Distribute resources equitably – ensure that resources at their disposal are distributed fairly, according to need.
4. Challenge unjust policies and practices – bring to the attention of their employers, policy makers, politicians and the general public situations where resources are inadequate or where distribution of resources, policies and practices are oppressive, unfair or harmful.
5. Working in solidarity – challenge social conditions that contribute to social exclusion, stigmatisation or subjugation and work towards an inclusive society.

These five aspects of social justice, as defined by IFSW (2005), highlight that social work is not merely about facilitating individual, or even familial, change, but rather should include a type of practice that penetrates into society in order to challenge existing barriers that prohibit individuals, families and communities from meeting their needs while equally recognising diversity within society and how needs are unique to individuals, families and communities. As such, the definition of social justice can be defined as 'distributing resources in society according to need (as opposed to desert or merit), challenging existing power structures and oppressive institutions and actions' (Banks, 2006, p 39). As this definition suggests, aiming for social justice requires social workers to tackle discrimination and oppression and to distribute resources to those in need at a societal and environmental level, which in some situations may involve the global community or environment.

Globalisation

A global community does not necessarily equate with globalisation, and social work in a global community does not necessarily support globalisation. Globalisation is defined as 'the process by which all peoples and communities come to experience an increasingly common economic, social and cultural environment' (IFSW, 2005). Several theorists have argued that globalisation is a threat or seen as the end to communities; for example, Hardcastle (2004) argues that globalisation, which involves a non-regulated market, breaks down communities as the corporations participating in capitalism have no interest in social welfare programmes. This definition and approach to globalisation could be a threat to social work and to individuals and groups in need as the push for one society, dominated by capitalism, will result in one prominent culture with rules and norms defined by the most powerful in the global society. This could result in a lack of defined diversity and a sense of local or national communities. Alternatively, globalisation can be viewed as a trend towards international interdependence and integration (van Wormer and Besthorn, 2011). This perspective could work in alliance with social work values by combining resources and assets, knowledge and ideas in an attempt to meet the needs of the global society members, particularly those whose needs are not being met, while simultaneously respecting and appreciating diversity.

According to van Wormer and Besthorn (2011, p 201), 'globalization in itself is neither good nor bad; or, broadly speaking, it is both good and bad'. The extent to which globalisation is a positive or negative occurrence solely depends on the extent to which the community members of the global society feel valued and supported, their views and cultures respected and their needs met. Positive globalisation involves concentrating attention on the welfare of citizens versus corporate welfare (see Sewpaul, 2004), and such positive aspects to globalised work include women's rights, human rights and children's rights. The Earth Charter (2011), discussed in more detail below, is a strong and positive example of the sense of globalisation as a global community, which values and respects diversity. It upholds the following stance:

> We stand at a critical moment in Earth's history, a time when humanity must choose its future. As the world becomes increasingly interdependent and fragile, the future at once holds great peril and great promise. To move forward we must recognise that in the midst

of a magnificent diversity of cultures and life forms we are one human family and one Earth community with a common destiny. We must join together to bring forth a sustainable global society founded on respect for nature, universal human rights, economic justice, and a culture of peace. Towards this end, it is imperative that we, the peoples of Earth, declare our responsibility to one another, to the greater community of life, and to future generations. (The Earth Charter Initiative, 2011, p 1)

Exercise box 7.1: Globalisation and social work in a global community

In pairs or small groups, discuss the following:

1. What are the advantages and disadvantages to globalisation?
2. How might globalisation and social work in a global community be linked? How might they be separate?
3. Discuss the extent to which social workers should be concerned with globalisation.

Social work in the global community: approaches to practice

Communities have been argued to extend along a continuum, from local to global. A global community exists via a geographical area with the visible boundary of the earth. It equally exists as a functional community, sharing resources and the physical and built environment among community members. Given the importance placed on communities within social work practice, the global community should equally be seen as a client source for social workers who are working from a macro or political, global environmental or international level. In conducting this type of social work practice, social workers need to adhere to established approaches that seek to reap a particular aim among this client group (for example, eliminate poverty, reduce disease and illness or promote the human rights of women and children). This chapter focuses on two prominent and established approaches that are closely related and inter dependent – sustainable development and progressive change – and provides some examples of current initiatives that fall under each of these approaches.

Sustainable development

Sustainable development involves the sustainable integration of social, economic and environmental well-being (Hall and Midgley, 2004; Gamble and Weil, 2010). The approach was conceptualised in 1987 by the World Commission on Environment and Development (WCED) (commissioned by the UN) through their work on the exploration of the relationship between social development and the state of the world's natural environment (Gamble and Hoff, 2005). This approach can be closely aligned to social work practice as it firmly supports the social work theories that acknowledge individuals within their environments and the interactions and interdependence between the two systems (for example, social systems theory, person-in-environment and an ecological perspective). Sustainable development not only acknowledges and considers the social environment, but equally considers the effect of the economic and natural environment on human growth and development, and views these resources as viable to meet the needs of humans and to protect global resources (Gamble and Hoff, 2005).

According to Gamble and Hoff (2005), the concept of sustainable development is often closely aligned with the concepts of social development and human development. Although often seen as overlapping, they are also viewed as contradictory. Social development emerged after the Second World War when many countries were liberated from colonisation and were faced with the challenge of improving and maintaining the well-being of their citizens while simultaneously moving towards economic development (Midgley, 1995). Social development involved the overlap of social and economic well-being to the point that social services were viewed as an investment in economic development. Additionally, the active participation of citizens in developing and implementing programmes were viewed as critical to economic success (Gamble and Hoff, 2005).

Human development was first devised and measured in 1990 through the first *Human Development Report* by the UNDP. Human development is held to pertain to all countries, whether developed or developing, and is seen to:

> ... bring[s] together the production and distribution of commodities and the expansion and use of human capabilities. It also focuses on choices – on what people should have, be and do to be able to ensure their own livelihood. Human development is, moreover, concerned not only with basic needs satisfaction but also with human development as a participatory and dynamic process. It applies equally to less developed and highly developed countries. (UNDP, 2010, p 12)

The *1990 Human Development Report* also included the newly devised composite index to measure human development (UNDP, 2010), the Human Development Index (HDI), which was created by Mahbub ul-Haq of Pakistan and Amartya Sen of India. The index serves as a more accurate measure of national development, including other measures alongside national income, and the first *Human Development Report*, published in 1990, began with the phrase, 'people are the real wealth of the nation' (UDNP, 2010). The HDI included such additional measures of the development of people across developed and developing countries by considering three specific areas: (1) a long and healthy life, such as life expectancy at birth; (2) knowledge, as defined by adult literacy and school enrolment; and (3) a decent standard of living, as defined by adjusted per capita income (UNDP, 2010). The HDI serves as a basic tool for measuring sustainable community development and can also serve as a resource for social workers engaged in community practice to assist in evaluating the level of human development within a particular country or region (Gamble and Hoff, 2005). Both the concepts of social and human development are highlighted through the discussion on sustainable development below.

Sustainable development aims to foster human growth and development in a more holistic way by attempting to alleviate social and economic disparities while simultaneously protecting people, resources and the environment. This approach has a dual focus on the social and economic environment, built and maintained by humans, and on the physical environment, on which humans and all living creatures depend (Estes, 1993). According to the former Prime Minister of Norway, Gro Harlem Brundtland, sustainable development is the 'paths of human progress which meet the needs and aspirations of the present generation without compromising the ability of future generations to meet their needs' (WCED, 1987, p 2).

Individuals and organisations involved in sustainable development initiatives range from local entrepreneurs and farmers to large multinational corporations to cities and countries. On a global level, in 2000 the UN, with 189 heads of state and government, adopted the Millennium Declaration and developed Millennium Development Goals (MDGs) which have been recognised as the first step towards achieving sustainable development by 2015 (UN, 2011). Table 7.1 lists the eight MDGs for the 2015 target, which range from eradicating extreme poverty and hunger to improving maternal health to ensuring environmental sustainability. The Goals have been widely received and supported by NGOs as well as national non-profit organisations, such as the International Labour Organization, World Health Organization, United Nations Children's Fund (Unicef) and the Organisation for Economic Co-operation and Development, but there is still a great need for a positive response and commitment of aid and financial assistance from more developed countries in order for the MDGs to be achieved (UN, 2011).

In addition to the established MDGs, the UN has evaluated the extent to which nations across the globe are achieving sustainable development. In particular, the evaluation considered human development as measured by the HDI (as previously stated on page 99, the HDI measures three aspects of a nation's performance, on health, education and basic economic standards). The evaluation is published annually as the *Human Development Report*. This report more accurately reflects the performance of a nation by considering human, environmental and economic factors versus relying merely on economic factors, such as the measure of gross domestic product (GDP). Although GDP is a widely used and often cited measure of development, it only relies on measurable and available economic measures and fails to include those economic resources that are not often measured in terms of money, such as voluntary work or communal exchanges of services (Gamble and Weil, 2010). Table 7.2 lists the top 15 nations as measured by the HDI – the country with the highest HDI rank is Norway, followed closely by Australia. The UK is ranked 26th, with an HDI of 0.849 as reported in 2011. Sustainable development is, therefore, consistent with the holistic approach adopted by social work as it considers the ability of a nation to reach sustainability through the extent to which the nation improves social, economic and environmental well-being. Social well-being is seen to include the ability to have supportive relationships with families, friends, communities and neighbourhoods alongside access to health, welfare, security, political organisations, spiritual institutions and educational resources (Couto and Guthrie, 1999; Gamble and Weil, 2010). Economic well-being is evidenced by a way of life or livelihood that is not reliant merely on jobs but an ability for people to live a life that is meaningful to them, while having a wage that meets needs for themselves and for their families (Gamble and Weil, 2010). Economic well-being includes a healthy flow of supply and demand of goods and services, whether they are regulated by a market or more informal through exchange systems. Exchange systems do not necessarily establish a value on a good or service but represent the agreed patterns of activities to trade services and commodities, with a varying value placed on the service or commodity (for example, a work of art or childcare services offered by family members) (Gamble and Weil, 2010). Finally, environmental well-being includes natural or finite resources, often termed 'natural capital', such as water, food, soil, oxygen or other aspects of nature, and the ability to retain and preserve such resources for future generations (Hart, 1999).

The aspects of the holistic approach of social, economic and environmental well-being is congruent with the values and principles of social work, which views the person within their social and physical environment. Therefore, sustainable development may be appropriate for social workers in several ways. For example, social workers may collaborate with a local community to evaluate the existence of resources and explore the best ways in which community members could have access to such resources (such as keeping lakes and the local water supply clean for food and recreational fishing or developing a piece of land in which to have a communal garden). Gamble and Hoff (2005, p 7) provide the following initial questions that could guide social workers collaborating with communities towards sustainable development: (1) How will goals be agreed on that can sustain human development (for example, jobs, recreation, housing, transportation, cultural and religion diversity) while respecting the limits and natural character of a region? (2) How can social and economic development be planned so that it will not deplete natural resources beyond the natural restorative capacities of the region? An example of such work is provided by Matsuoka and McGregor (1994, as cited in Gamble and Hoff, 2005), which involves a Hawaiian juvenile delinquency programme aiming to restore Hawaiian cultural relationships to the land and sea to reduce delinquent behaviour among the Hawaiian youth.

The practice of sustainable development is anti-oppressive in nature and supports a participative approach. Social workers should be mindful of including as many voices as possible in sustainable development work, and should seek to promote the voices of the marginalised members, which can often include black and minority ethnic people, women and children. The relationship between social workers and community members should be one of collaboration and equality – personal and communal ownership of the work is more likely to lead to a successful development of sustainability. Gamble and Hoff (2005) advise social workers to adhere to a basic set of values as originally defined by Falk (1972, p 176): (1) unity of humankind and of life on earth; (2) minimisation of violence; (3) maintenance of environmental quality; (4) satisfaction of minimum world welfare standards; (5) primacy of human dignity; (6) retention of diversity and pluralism; and (7) the need for universal participation.

Keeping these seven basic values in mind, we now turn to the basic process of sustainable development work. This process, provided by Gamble and Weil (2010, p 217), consists of 10 guiding steps that, although presented in a linear fashion, can actually occur in various orders depending on the needs and experiences within the community. The ability to be flexible and to have a flexible approach is just as important as the steps that follow:

1. *Identify and establish a working relationship with a neighbourhood or community group that has concerns for social, economic and/or environmental issues.* This can begin with a dialogue about the most pressing issues for the community, analysing the problems and coming to a mutual understanding that the social, economic and environmental problems may be linked. The goal is to identify one or two problems as the focus

of the work versus problems from the three main areas (social, economic and environmental).

2. *Assess the leadership and organisational assets and challenges within the neighbourhood or community using popular education and participatory appraisal techniques.* This can involve bringing the community members together to plan collectively as to how they will solve the problem, in particular using the resources and assets that they already possess. Community members will need to be engaged, they will need to participate, and to take ownership of the solutions to the problems.

3. *Help the neighbourhood or community to deepen their understanding of sustainable development by exploring with them how their work towards improved social and/or economic outcomes is necessarily linked to environmental conditions, or how their work to improve environmental conditions is necessarily linked to social and economic outcomes.* This involves educating community members about how their actions and efforts have knock-on improvements in other aspects of their community. For example, removing rubbish from ponds and rivers could lead to an environmental improvement, but also a social improvement by providing cleaner areas for children and families to use for recreational activities, and an economic improvement by enabling the use of the water for fishing and agricultural purposes.

4. *Assist the neighbourhood or community to develop techniques for setting goals and objectives for improving their community that integrates improved social, economic, and environmental outcomes.* This involves the continual education of community members of the connection between social, economic and environmental aspects and encouraging solutions to the problems to consider the immediate and knock-on effects for each of these three areas. A solution should not be implemented without considering how it will have an impact on the social, economic and environmental aspects of the community.

5. *Assist the neighbourhood or community organisation leaders to develop skills for forming alliances, acquiring resources and employing wide and inclusive communication systems.* The focus should be on enhancing the social, economic and environmental well-being of each member of the community, which should involve using and building on existing resources and relationships, and also further strengthening the resources and relationships in order for all community members to have a better quality of life that builds on their potential.

6. *Assist the neighbourhood or community organisation to think through strategies for reaching their goals and objectives in ways that empower and build the capacity of both primary and secondary leadership.* Relationships, alliances and leadership are critical in order to reach sustainable development. Identifying and implementing solutions needs the involvement of private, public, non-profit and interest-affiliated groups.

7. *Assist the neighbourhood or community to learn how to manage internal conflict and disagreement as their organisation grows and confronts new challenges.* All community members should be valued and treated with respect and the leaders of the sustainable development movement should be collaborative and transparent with community members.

8. *Assist the neighbourhood or community organisation in learning how to monitor and evaluate the progress of their effort and to share those outcomes inside and outside the community.* Collecting baseline data on variables that are important to the community (such as literacy rates, life expectancy, poverty rate and school education) can assist the community in determining any successes and improvements that may not always be visible.

9. *Assist the neighbourhood or community organisations to plan for and take effective action.* Such action must be within the immediate future, but is also required in order to sustain improvements and to continue them into the future.

10. *Assist the organisation to plan celebrations that mark the progress of leadership, organisational development, milestone outcomes and action victories.* Celebrations of success can continue to fuel the desire to sustain the changes, improvements and milestones that have been achieved. Communities should celebrate such successes as well as the efforts of the community members themselves.

The work of sustainable development initiatives can be evaluated through the collection and analysis of community indicators, such as quality-of-life indicators, which can be collected at baseline and then monitored in the following years. On a global level, this information is already being collected for each country, through the UN *Human Development Report*, and is readily available to social workers and other community workers who want to evaluate changes to the quality-of-life indicators (such as human development, poverty and gender development) (Gamble and Hoff, 2005).

Progressive change

Progressive change is a similar concept, process and aim as sustainable development. It seeks to tackle and revolutionise negative conditions within communities, whether local, regional or global, in an attempt to produce improved social, economic and environmental outcomes for the most disadvantaged populations (Gamble and Weil, 2010). Progressive change places a particular emphasis on working with community members who are less likely to have a voice in decision making and who are often excluded based on gender, ethnicity, ability, age, religion or sexual preference.

It involves a community taking itself to a higher level in regard to social, economic, political and environmental well-being with the community, defining exactly what 'progressive' change would mean to them (Gamble and Weil, 2010). As noted above, when discussing sustainable development, social well-being involves the ability to have supportive relationships and access to social and welfare resources; economic well-being includes having a livelihood that is meaningful and a wage that is sufficient; and environmental well-being includes having access to natural capital, such as water, soil and oxygen, and preserving these resources for future generations. An additional aspect to progressive change is political well-being, which involves the ability of people to participate in governmental decisions through having a voice and an ability to cast a vote (Gamble and Weil, 2010).

Progressive change promotes social, economic and environmental justice. This practice can take place on an individual, community, national or international level. For example, Estes (1993) reports seven strategic levels in which social workers and/or community activists can intervene in order to promote social, economic and environmental justice, which include: (1) individual and group empowerment; (2) conflict resolution; (3) community building; (4) institution building; (5) national building; (6) region building; and (7) world building.

An international example of a progressive change initiative involves the Earth Charter, which 'formulates principles that will guide a nation's transition from a system that exploits people and resources to a system that promotes sustainable development, and thus provides a global road map for change' (Gamble and Weil, 2010, p 16). It was created as a follow-up to the 1992 Earth Summit, with the goal of creating a census as to the values and principles that would lead to a sustainable future. Over 5,000 people contributed to its development and it is now endorsed by thousands of organisations, including international NGOs as well as international governmental bodies. The Earth Charter outlines four main principles:

1. *Respect and care for the community of life* – this includes respecting and valuing all forms of life, protecting the rights of people and promoting the common good, promoting social and economic well-being, and transmitting values to future generations and ensuring that these generations are able to use economic resources.
2. *Ecological integrity* – this includes protecting and restoring the Earth's ecological systems that present harm to the ecological system by reducing, reusing and recycling and relying on renewable energy sources.
3. *Social and economic justice* – this includes eradicating poverty, promoting human development and sustainability, ensuring access to healthcare, education and economic opportunity and eliminating discrimination in all its forms.

4.   *Democracy, non-violence and peace* – this includes promoting the interest of individuals and organisations in decision making and access to justice, treating all living beings with respect and consideration and promoting a culture of tolerance, non-violence and peace (The Earth Charter Initiative, 2011, pp 2-5).

The Earth Charter's four principles compliment the aims and objectives of social work practice, from promoting human rights and social justice, to considering the environment of clients and the interactions between person and community and environment. The following details two examples of good practice from the Earth Charter (Earth Charter International, 2010), with the main aims consistent with the aims of social work practice.

COPE project. The COPE project operates on the Earth Charter's principle, to 'eradicate poverty as an ethical, social, and environmental imperative' (The Earth Charter Initiative, 2011, p 3). It takes place in Zambia and involves a 20-year plan to eliminate rural poverty through the creation and use of a contentment economy using traditional cultural village practices. The project leaders believe that health problems must be eliminated by using sustainable methods, such as solar and fuel-efficient cooking, water purification and waterless toilets. The gains that would be saved through health and labour practices would then be used for education, organising women's social groups, the expansion of small-scale agriculture and the stimulation of local economies. The villages have been trained to carry out the project and have agreed to assist in training other villages (Earth Charter International, 2010, p 6).

Earth Charter Youth Groups (ECYGs). There are currently more than 90 ECYGs in over 100 countries, which are characterised as dynamic action-oriented youth groups promoting the principles of the Earth Charter among young people. One particular group, called Rafique Research and Educational ECYG, is located in Pakistan and sought to take action after the devastating floods in 2010 to help the country's internally displaced people. The group was able to fundraise in order to help more than 1,100 people in their home community of Lodhran through providing food and medicine. ECYGs involve young people studying and getting inspired by the Earth Charter's declaration and principles and they then organise small action projects to promote justice, sustainability and peace within their local communities (Earth Charter International, 2010, p 8).

Global role of civil society organisations and non-governmental organisations

Both CSOs and NGOs have established a significant presence across the globe over the past decade. In 2006, it was estimated that there were more than 50,000 international NGOs, with CSOs providing more than US$15 billion in international assistance (The World Bank, 2010). CSOs are particularly significant in delivering social services and development programmes, and are defined as:

> [T]he wide array of non-governmental and not-for-profit organizations that have a presence in public life, expressing the interests and values of their members or others, based on ethical, cultural, political, scientific, religious or philanthropic considerations. Civil Society Organizations (CSOs) therefore refer to a wide of array of organizations: community groups, non-governmental organizations (NGOs), labor unions, indigenous groups, charitable organizations, faith-based organizations, professional associations, and foundations. (The World Bank, 2010)

NGOs fall under the auspice of CSOs and tend to be non-profit or voluntary citizens' group organisations that may be organised and operating at a local, national or international level. They bring people together who have a common interest and/or common cause (such as human rights, environment or health), and work together to provide service and humanitarian functions and to advocate and monitor policies (NGO Global Network, 2011).

Participation in CSOs and NGOs has become more prominent in low- and middle-income countries, and the development of such voluntary associations are enabling communities to respond to local needs, to promote sustainable development and to engage in decision making (Gamble and Weil, 2010). CSOs have empowerment as the core of their work, and when recently surveyed by Human Development Report Organisation staff, they (94 per cent of all CSOs) ranked the following as the most important dimensions of empowerment (UNDP, 2010, p 115): (1) literacy and education (66 per cent); (2) right to vote (54 per cent); (3) freedom of expression (52 per cent); (4) choosing one's own destiny (35 per cent); (5) making personal choices (33 per cent); (6) decision making in home (29 per cent); (7) joining voice with others (27 per cent); (8) protesting (19 per cent); (9) standing or running for elected office (18 per cent); and (10) group identity (12 per cent).

The importance of CSOs and NGOs is the ability of citizens to participate in society and to have collective agency and action. The UNDP (2002, p 53) emphasised the importance of citizen participation through democratic governance, and argued that, 'collective action through social and political movements has often been a motor of progress for issues central to human development: protecting the environment, promoting gender equality, fostering human rights'. This type of citizen participation is at the core of community practice and social work in the community. In this regard, community members have a sense of freedom as citizens are able to collectively define problems, needs and solutions – free from governmental agendas, yet with the ability to penetrate into and work alongside such agendas.

Summary and conclusion

This chapter has argued that communities range from a local to a global level and social workers should be knowledgeable of the approaches to practice that range across this continuum. Social work aims to promote social justice, empowerment and the liberation of people to enhance well-being. Including a global perspective could only enhance opportunities for individuals, groups and communities to be liberated from oppression, discrimination and inequalities and to experience true freedom. According to the UNDP (2000, p 1), there are seven basic universal freedoms that ensure an individual's well-being, security and human dignity. These include:

- freedom from discrimination
- freedom from want
- freedom to develop and fully realise human potential
- freedom from fear
- freedom from injustice and violations of the rule of law
- freedom of thought and speech
- freedom to engage in decent work without exploitation.

These freedoms are synonymous with the values of social work as they embody the values of social and economic justice and basic human rights (Gamble and Weil, 2010), and they are the aims of several international initiatives, such as the MDGs and the Earth Charter.

Social work practice within a global context does not necessarily mean support for globalisation, but rather support for those international organisations that promote the social, economic and environmental well-being of individuals while simultaneously valuing difference and diversity. This chapter has looked at sustainable development and progressive change as two linked approaches that could be used in a global context, and also explored the importance and relevance of CSOs and NGOs. Such global knowledge points to the relevance of social workers becoming acquainted with roles and activities that take place on an international level that seek to promote social, economic and environmental well-being. As Ife (2007) has argued, all social workers should understand the scope and causes of poverty and inequality worldwide, yet this emphasis is not always existent within Western educational institutions or social work practice. Ife (2007, p 12) argues that this trend must change:

> It is the obscenity of global poverty, and the unequal distribution of global resources, that make international social work so necessary and so difficult, and that result in the massive lack of resources to provide adequate health care, housing, education and employment for the people of the Global South. But how can we do international social work if at home we define social work in such a way that poverty and inequality are not longer its core concerns? I would suggest that if social work education is to equip social workers to work internationally, a thorough study of poverty and inequality, nationally and globally, and a rediscovery of our profession's historical commitment, is fundamental.

This broadened understanding places poverty, inequality, social justice and humanitarian issues outside of a local and regional level, and extends it to the international or global level. Creating a global community will create a sense that poverty, inequality and social justice on a global level is the responsibility of social workers all over the world. Social workers should start this approach to practice at a local level where they become interested and concerned in issues that extend beyond their regional boundaries, and begin to see the globe as one community.

The future of social work practice in the community: making a difference

8

Introduction

This book has attempted to demonstrate the importance of social work practice in the community and this has been illustrated through the use of three case examples of social work practice in both the statutory and voluntary sectors. The social work practice by Hasan, Anna, Irene and Jenny are indicative of social work practice in the community that truly seeks to see individuals in their environment and the necessity of identifying and addressing individual and collective needs. These practice examples should provide evidence for the relevance of communities to social work practice, and illustrate the way in which social workers can carry out practice that is purely aligned to the aims and values of social work and the international definition of social work practice.

Social work practice in the community takes the focus of social work prevention and intervention away from concentrating solely on the individual, and widens this perspective to include the individual in his or her environment as well as the collective needs of individuals. This approach sits firmly with the definition of social work produced by the IASSW and the IFSW (as discussed in Chapter Seven) and challenges an individualistic approach that seeks to reduce or eliminate difficulties faced by individuals by acknowledging that individuals are continually affected by their environment, which includes relationships, communities and society. We argue that social work is not just about working with individuals to alleviate problems or difficulties – it is about working with individuals, families, groups and communities to identify individual and collective needs and to alleviate individual and collective difficulties. This wider more social perspective is congruent with the promotion of social justice in assessing and exploring societal expectations, norms and power structures, and the influence of these societal factors on individuals, families, groups and communities. This is in contrast to an individualistic approach that assesses how an individual can change or adapt to alleviate difficulties that may more appropriately lie within a much bigger structure (such as community or society) that is out of his or her control; thus, social justice is less of a focus within the individualist approach. Social work practice in the community is therefore congruent with the international definition of social work, which includes 'community' throughout, and is one way of working to promote social justice.

This concluding chapter seeks to summarise the main issues presented in this book by providing a rationale and support for including 'community' in social work practice. The future outlook for social work practice in a community context is discussed by exploring the strengths and weaknesses of practising social work in the community and by considering the theories, values and ethics as well as the political and organisational factors affecting social work practice within communities, as discussed in earlier chapters.

Social work practice in the community

Why specifically social work practice in the community? As the practice examples in this book have illustrated, considering the collective needs of a community produces benefits to both individuals and the environment in which they live, and specifically their communities. A community-based approach to social work practice focuses on preventive methods rather than just merely intervening when problems or difficulties arise, which builds on the community's already existing strengths and resources and the supportive relationships that may already exist. Building on such strengths and resources empowers communities to address needs and potentially prevent problems and difficulties from arising in the future, or at least have the knowledge, skills, strengths and resources identified in order to combat problems and difficulties when they do emerge. Such an approach values the social and collective and not just the individual, thus promoting a supportive environment rather than one that could be isolating. Additionally, social work in the community starts from the premise that broader social, economic and political factors, such as discrimination, oppression, poverty and social, political and economic exclusion, influence and have an impact on the individual within that community, and any problems or difficulties that arise for individuals and families may be attributed to these factors. Taking a broader perspective on social work practice enables social workers to identify the true source of the problem and to intervene in the appropriate area or system as well as to assist communities in mobilising their strengths and resources to combat such problems or difficulties if they should occur. Again, social work practice in the community highlights the commitment of social work to promote social justice by viewing the interrelations and interconnections between personal problems and the broader social and political structures (Mendes, 2009).

Social work practice in the community is not a new concept or approach and can be implemented in several ways. This book has highlighted the ways in which social work practice in the community could be conducted, such as community development, community action, community social work and community needs assessment or community profiling. Community development involves mobilising groups to come together, to build on their strengths and to promote services within their local area (Payne, 2005); community action consists of advocating for services and seeking change directly from the political decision makers and influential groups in the community (Payne, 2005); community social work strives to work in partnership with communities seeking a more collective voice versus a focus on social workers as individual consumers (Barclay, 1982) and community needs assessments or community profiling involves identifying and assessing the needs and wants of a community, particularly with the active involvement of the community members themselves (Hawtin and Percy-Smith, 2007). Additionally, legislation, legislative frameworks and policy guidance documents also require or encourage assessment of community needs (such as the Children Act 1989), assessment of the impact of community services or systems on individuals and families (that is, community care) and/or the involvement of the community in identifying and assessing needs (*Our health, our care, our say*; *Putting people first*). So social work practice in the community is not a new or specifically radical approach but rather an approach that is implemented and acknowledged to varying degrees by social work practice, political decision makers and legislation and policy documents.

Social work in the community is, as we have argued, heavily consistent with general social work practice, so the practice of social work in the community is acknowledged and stressed among current-day social work practice. Social work theories and methods consistently stress the acknowledgement and assessment of the person in his or her environment. For example, social systems theory stresses the assessment of the interactions and interconnectedness of the person in their environment and the need to determine where interventions are most appropriately directed (such as individual, family, school, social services or government policy). The strengths perspective and empowerment approach both call for an assessment of individual, interpersonal, communal and societal strengths and resources, and how implementing the empowerment-based approach with an individual may not necessarily work if the individual is experiencing discrimination, oppression, stigma or exclusion from a broader system, such as the community or society. Anti-discriminatory practice and anti-oppressive practice, most prevalent in modern-day social work practice, requires an analysis of social, economic and political factors on individuals, families and communities. For example, Thompson's (2006) PCS (personal, cultural, structural) model stresses how the person is embedded within a culture within their society, and that all three must be acknowledged and assessed. And, as stressed within the international definition of social work, social justice is a key aim of social work practice and is simply impossible to assess or promote within an individualistic approach alone.

Importance of defining need

Need, as we see it, is defined as physical health (consistent with basic human needs) and personal and critical autonomy (Doyal and Gough, 1991), where personal autonomy is congruent with human dignity and the opportunity to have a voice in decisions that affects an individual's life, with critical autonomy involving the ability to individually or collectively 'question and to participate in agreeing and changing the rules' (Doyal and Gough, 1991, p 67). Therefore, when assessing need as a critical part of social work assessment and practice, it is important to identify and assess both individual and collective need. Collective need can either be collective in the sense of those residing within a geographical area, or those individuals who share a common characteristic or trait. In keeping with anti-oppressive and anti-discriminatory practice, the assessment of need must include those of the individual as well as of the collective, particularly in ensuring that minority views are heard and the determination of need is not based on 'majority rules', which would oppress the unique views of those in the minority.

Therefore, the use of community profiles is viewed as most appropriate for identifying and assessing need, particularly through its requirement for involvement from community members and its commitment to reaching and seeking the views of all community members, especially those who may be marginalised. As illustrated in Chapter Six, community profiles can be useful in identifying the strengths, resources and needs of a community and implementing services or using and building on existing strengths and resources to address needs and prevent future problems. In this sense, community profiles serve as a form of preventive social work practice. Community profiles are also useful when conducting research or an evaluation of a service or programme. It can build a picture of a community, the community's needs and an evidence base on which to make judgements about where and when to implement or provide services, now and in the future. Community profiles serve a useful purpose for statutory agencies where community data and needs assessments are required by legislation or to support where and when services are allocated. Additionally, community profiles are useful to voluntary agencies in determining service delivery and also supporting the requirement for funding to provide services in the community to meet particular identified needs.

Need is also an important concept for community social work and for community development, which was addressed in Chapters Four and Five. In addition to needs in communities, we also emphasised the importance of strengths and resources in communities, and highlighted the informal networks within communities that serve as a source of support for the majority of people. For example, community social work, as a way of thinking about social work practice (Barclay Committee, 1982), would argue that people with learning difficulties, in one of the practice examples, and their friends, family carers and neighbours, could be seen as a network of potential reciprocal relationships. The more these informal supports can be nurtured and the longer they can be maintained, the less likely social workers will have to resort to dealing with crises, resulting in better situations for service users, their family carers and for their communities. Community social work can also enable social workers to get back to positive creative social work practice.

Community profiling, community social work and community development also remind us how important it is for us as social workers to find out about the expressed needs of communities. We noted that the processes in which communities and the individuals within them can voice their concerns and opinions have positive effects on those people. Many people in working-class communities, within which social workers generally practise, are not used to being listened to – young people, older people with dementia, people with mental health problems or people with learning difficulties. Real involvement can make people feel valued and that they have a voice in how their needs are met. This can be very empowering and bring people into supportive communities rather than excluding them. Social workers could take steps to make their presence known more in the communities where they practise. In conjunction with other statutory organisations, they could run public meetings to hear the voices of communities and then feed these expressed needs into decision-making processes in their organisations. Group work is rare but not unheard of in professional social work practice. Group work that gives people a voice, raises their consciousness about their individual and collective experience and gives them the opportunity for mutual support will have the effect of empowering people – giving back some control in their lives. Putting on events, maybe in participation with a community arts organisation, can be a way into the lives of disaffected young people that would give them a voice and social workers visibility in the community.

A host of practical ideas have been presented within this book but all require, for statutory social workers in particular, sanction from managers, and rigorous systems of workload management to protect some of their time to engage in these practices. The evidence that there is as far as prevention is concerned suggests that this would be time and resources well spent. Social work in the community can make a real difference in people's lives, steering them away from crisis and keeping them where they want to be – within their communities.

Social work in the community: strengths and limitations

Social work practice in the community can take various forms and be viewed as both preventive and intervention-based, although it is primarily preventive in nature. This type of social work practice has a number of limitations, which are detailed below:

- Social workers may find this approach to practice difficult within their agency or organisation, due to time, resources and some practices that require an *individualistic approach*. They may find themselves in agencies where they have a high caseload and specific tasks to complete that are often individual-based and focused on crises. They may not have the time it takes to engage with the community or community members in order to identify and assess collective need in addition to individual need. Additionally, they may not have the support from agencies to take a community or preventive focus when they are also struggling to meet legislative criteria or targets.
- Shifting mainstream social work practice from a focus on individuals to a more holistic approach requires a substantial *shift in attitude* by practitioners, managers and politicians. Such a shift will be very hard to achieve given the depth of individualism as an ideology in the consciousness of these key players. While this does not undermine the importance of working to affect a shift in hearts and minds, it does point to the magnitude of the task ahead.
- The *intervention-based approach* operating in some agencies, primarily the statutory sector, does not provide an environment for preventive-based work. Social work, particularly in a statutory agency, is often dictated by legislation that treats practice as primarily intervention-based versus preventive. For example, the NHS and Community Care Act 1990 and FACS requires social workers to assess the level of need of the service user, and then social services are generally only able to provide services to those most in need (that is, those with substantial or critical need). This type of intervention-based work limits the amount of preventive work that social workers can do, particularly in communities, when the focus of services tends to be on the individual and responding to individual crises.

Additionally, social work practice has identified strengths, which are detailed below:

- Social work practice in the community is viewed as *preventive* in nature. When working collaboratively with community members to identify and define needs, the community's strengths and resources are also being identified and assessed and can be built on and used to address the identified need. Building on the tools already present within the community can serve as a preventive measure for future problems arising. When needs are identified and addressed, future problems can then be eliminated or greatly reduced.

- Social work practice in the community, by adopting a community orientation as a way of understanding social problems, fits neatly with the developmental practice of *critical reflection* (Fook, 2002) which is widely considered to be a key aspect of what makes social work the unique profession that it is. Community can be a key aspect, not just of a critical reflective approach but also of an evaluative approach. For example, when reflecting on our own individual practice, we can ask ourselves whether we are taking the broader context of community into account when assessing the needs of *this* family or individual. To see only the individual is often to perpetuate the problem of the individual by adding to his or her experience of stigma and oppression. It is also a tool for critical reflection and evaluation of agency practice, should we ask what needs are being assumed by *this* organisation in providing *this* service. Could we, from a community perspective, see these needs in a more collective way, and would we then also consider services in a different way?

- Social work practice in the community is congruent with social work values, theories and the purpose of social work, as defined through the international definition of social work. Social work practice in the community is based on the theories of *social systems, strengths perspective* and the *empowerment approach*, all of which assess the individual, family, group or community within the environment and the interconnectedness and interdependence among these systems. Taking a holistic perspective enables social work practice to promote social justice by acknowledging how individual problems can actually be caused by factors on a much larger scale, such as discrimination, oppression, poverty, stigma and exclusion.

The future of social work in the community

We return, at this point, to the arguments made in earlier chapters, when it was noted that how we understand things determines how we then deal with them. These are sociological arguments about knowledge, and what counts as truth in the social world. We have discussed theories of discourse and social constructivism, so readers should be aware that we are not interested in merely accepting the powerful ways of making sense of the social work world but in also understanding how one version rather than another holds sway.

In mainstream social work it is not community perspectives that inform social work practice but individualism. Individualism is an ideology that is deeply embedded within white Western culture. In an excellent essay written in 1974, at a time when community work was much more talked about and practised, the philosopher, Plant (1974), endeavoured to make sense of the concept of community in a society obsessed with individualism. He argued persuasively that individualism originated from 17th and 18th-century thinkers who were keen to argue that the medieval notion of community was a problematic one, and one which deprived 'free persons' (Plant, 1974, p 30) of their right to free association. He noted that these writers successfully argued, in the emerging enlightenment and protestant catalyst for capitalist social and economic relationships, that it was 'free, self-conscious individuals who derived their freedom and consciousness of themselves precisely from the decline and loss of closer, communal forms of social relationship' (p 31). This argument is a powerful reminder of just how deeply embedded within 'our' culture this ideology of individualism is, and how easy it is for practitioners to default to thinking *only* of service users as individuals and not seeing them in their wider contexts of family, neighbourhood, community and society.

We see this obsession with a purely individual approach to identifying and dealing with troubles as problematic, and this book proposes an alternative to the problems created by individualism. This focus on the individual to the exclusion of their environmental surroundings is not just the natural order of things but an ideological approach. The policy drivers of giving choice to individual consumers within a market of care, and targeting those in most need, are not just (or even) common-sense approaches to the delivery of social welfare but policy and procedural responses to that ideology which, in itself, sits within a broader political framework of neoliberalism. Therefore, this is a very particular way of understanding and addressing social problems that, in fact, denies that they are *social* problems. A system that does not regard the structural factors that impinge on an individual's life does not then have to acknowledge that it is the political and economic system that creates inequalities, the casualties of which social work has to then support.

Rather, it is easier for such a system to focus on individual responsibility and to blame individuals for their circumstances. In addition, focusing on individual need and promoting individual choice in the services provided to meet that need will mean a system that is less concerned with the costly collective services that are rapidly disappearing across the UK in the wake of personalisation. Despite some of the problems of collective services, such as day and residential care, they are still the services that many people want, and which local communities are now beginning to champion and resist the closure of (Ferguson and Woodward, 2009).

Harris and White (2009) conclude their book on modernising social work by considering whether social work as it is currently organised in statutory settings has inextricably taken over the hearts and minds of social workers, service users, managers and students, or whether there is a recognition rather that we work within that system, but the system is not one that is meekly accepted. There is clearly evidence of alternative views (see, for example, Ferguson and Woodward, 2009), and we would like this book to be seen in that context. Social work in the community is a way of resisting that tendency in which 'neo-liberalism is now indelibly inscribed on the consciousness of service user, social workers and managers' (Harris and White, 2009, p 170).

Therefore, a social worker or student who advocates for a particular service user as a member of their broader community of need and who notes the collective nature of the poverty or discrimination that a particular family are experiencing or who insists on understanding and using the collective strengths and informal resources within communities is resisting that ideology that is currently dominating social work. We have argued that recognising and emphasising the social and collective as a set of values and not just the individual will result in a more supportive rather than isolating approach to individual service users. We have, in addition, noted that values that reflect the social rather than the economic are more likely to make a difference in marginalised people's lives, rather than just successfully managing scarce resources. Social work practice in the community is, we argue, more likely to be effective as well as economic. Not considering social work in the community and only dealing with individuals in crisis means failing those individuals. Social work is, then, not making a difference in any positive sense of the phrase. It has, to borrow from another radical campaign, become a part of the problem rather than a part of the solution.

Social work in the community certainly has a future as a critical alternative to current mainstream practice. We have not advocated the reintroduction of some of the historical approaches to the incorporation of community into social work in this book, so we are not saying 'bring back community development' or 'reintroduce community social work' – we seek to avoid describing a way of practising that is not feasible in contemporary social work organisations. The suggestions made in this book for more holistic practice are completely achievable in current organisations, assuming some shift in resources and, most obviously, a shift in attitude. What we are advocating is the importance of the knowledge, skills and values of a community orientation in making mainstream practice more effective, but to achieve this will require a paradigm shift in professional and managerial attitudes. How to affect that shift in perspective is perhaps the greatest challenge for anyone who would like to see a reintroduction of the 'social' into social work. We hope that the arguments in this book will be part of the persuasive process in shifting attitudes in behaviour change.

There are a number of positive examples of potential practice in this book that we feel fit the rubric of a more effective, engaged and holistic social work practice – social work practice in the community. We conclude by summarising these practical possibilities that, we believe, student social workers and professional practitioners could, often in partnership with service users and citizens within their communities, successfully attempt in the future. We would certainly welcome hearing about any examples of the suggestions below, or others, being introduced into mainstream social work practice, with an evaluation of their effectiveness. We believe that social work in the community has a sound practical future in mainstream social work as well as the rhetorical voice mentioned above.

Social work is about the art of the possible, within available resources, and we feel that the following are possible and will make a difference to the lives of marginalised individuals and communities:

■ *Take account of community resources* when dealing with individuals and do not only consider the needs and resources of atomised individuals. Most of us, in those difficult times of our lives, would look pretty helpless if our broader networks of support were not taken into consideration when the problems that beset us were assessed. For most service users, there are pressures of poverty, racism, disabling or ageist attitudes, homophobia, sexism and/or a denial of ethnic, religious and class culture. These are not just individual but collective experiences. Acknowledging them in this way is inclusive, not exclusive and isolating.

■ *Find the resources* (for example, from a student placement or from collaborating with a voluntary organisation) to carry out a community profile. Engaging with a community of interest or one of the geographical communities that your team visits could be a huge opportunity to learn about informal resources available. It demonstrates connection with the communities in which service users live and an interest and concern with their lives. These are hugely important factors for social workers who are often not thought to care much about the people with whom they work. A community profile improves knowledge of the area and can expel myths about the needs of a neighbourhood. It can also educate in the opposite direction, with the community understanding more about a social work team as they become more visible in the neighbourhood. As we saw from Chapter Six, a community profile can also produce an evaluation of a service provided which would mean that it could be developed, taking into consideration the voice of the people who actually use it to meet their needs. It is hard to oppose the fundamental logic of the argument that listening to what people express as their needs is likely to result in a more effective service to meet those needs.

■ *Networking*, as an approach to the communities of need and interest that social workers practise within, has a long tradition that has been more or less lost in mainstream statutory teams. Re-engaging with those networks, perhaps through links with voluntary organisations or service user-led organisations, could be a positive way of demonstrating interest in the expressed needs of communities and of sharing mutual interests in relation to specific issues. Seeking common agendas with such organisations could free up resources from both sides to put into more preventive work.

■ *Recording the unmet needs* from accumulated assessments of individuals provides potentially powerful information about the collective needs of communities. This practice, introduced in the community care and care management changes of the 1990s, has never really been considered important or useful by practitioners and teams. Collecting and collating such information would enable teams not only to understand the needs of the community that they are not meeting but would also provide powerful evidence to present to the controllers of resources in their organisations that could result in the shifting of resources in more effective directions.

■ Using such data within employer organisations is one aspect of our next practical possibility, that is, *advocating on behalf of community and collective needs*. Noting the collective nature of social problems such as poverty, ill health, racism, disability and ageism, emphasises that very often the behaviour associated with referral to statutory social work services is actually logical given the circumstances within which people have to cope with problems, rather than symptoms of pathology within the individual. This may change the assessment that a social worker makes of an individual's circumstances when it comes to advocating on their behalf with decision-making bodies such as courts, mental health tribunals or resource providers.

■ *Model collective action.* As the Barclay Committee noted (1982), the overwhelming majority of social problems are resolved within community and family networks. It would seem to be a very good thing for social work as a profession to model that collective, mutually aiding process, although we know that many social workers do not even receive supportive supervision from their line managers, let alone the mutual support of a team ethos. There are clearly exceptions to this, but working practices (working from home, desk-hopping, virtual offices) undermine the collective approach to social work that has proved so important to the support and collaborative learning approach to the profession's development. In addition, if we are to protect ourselves, as practitioners, from the potential negative effects of demonstrating that many of the social problems we deal with are socially constructed through the forces of discrimination, oppression and social injustice, then we too need to stick together for self-protection. Employment-focused organisations such as trades unions and broader-based organisations such as the Social Work Action Network (see www.socialworkfuture.org), a collective organisation for service users, social workers, students and academics, are important in this regard.

Somewhere along the way community, as a focus for practice, has become disassociated from mainstream social work practice. There is no logic, from either the profession's history or from its knowledge base and values, to maintain this separation. It is time for social work and social workers to re-engage with the concept of community in order to make a difference in the lives of the individuals who live marginalised lives. As argued above, we can return to our core values and remind ourselves that it is our role to make the social work, not the markets. However, the focus on individualism and eligibility for access to scarce resources means that social workers have become embroiled in a drive to make the market in care work and not the social. Refocusing on the social in social work involves, as an important, if not central, aspect, a refocus on community as a locus of need and of resources to deal with social problems.

References

Adams, R. (2008) *Empowerment, participation and social work* (4th edn), Basingstoke: Palgrave Macmillan.

Alinsky, S. (1971) *Rules for radicals: A pragmatic primer for realistic radicals*, New York: Vintage Books.

Andrews, A.B. and Motes, P.S. (2007) 'Organizational and community capacity building: mediating change in family-serving organizations and groups', in P.S. Motes and P.M. Hess (eds) *Collaborating with community-based organizations*, New York: Columbia University Press, pp 1-19.

Arnstein, R. (1969) 'A ladder of citizen participation', *Journal of the American Institute of Planners*, vol 35, no 4, pp 216-24.

Audit Commission (1992) *The community revolution: Managing the cascade of change*, London: HMSO.

Axford, N. (2010) 'Conducting Needs assessments in children's services', *British Journal of Social Work*, vol 40, no 1, pp 4-25.

Baldwin, M. (2000) *Care management and community care: Social work discretion and the construction of policy*, Aldershot: Ashgate.

Baldwin, M. (2002) 'New Labour and social care: continuity or change?', in M. Powell (ed) *Evaluating New Labour's welfare reforms*, Bristol: The Policy Press, pp 167-188.

Baldwin, M. (2006) 'Helping people with learning difficulties into paid employment: will UK social workers use the available welfare to work system?', *Journal of Policy Practice*, vol 5, no 2/3, pp 91-107.

Baldwin, M. (2008) 'Social care under Blair: are social care services more modern?', in M. Powell (ed) *Modernising the welfare state: The Blair legacy*, Bristol: The Policy Press, pp 73-90.

Baldwin, M. (2011) 'Resisting the EasyCare model: building a more radical, community-based, anti-authoritarian social work for the future', in M. Lavalette (ed) *Radical social work today: Social work at the crossroads*. Bristol: The Policy Press, pp 187-204.

Baldwin, M. and Sadd, J. (2006) 'Allies with attitude: service users, academics and social services agency staff learning how to share power in running a social work education course', *Social Work Education*, vol 25, no 4, pp 348-59.

Banks, S. (2006) *Ethics and values in social work* (3rd edn), Basingstoke: Palgrave Macmillan.

Barbour, R.S. and Kitzinger, J. (1999) *Developing focus group research: Politics, theory and practice*, London: Sage Publications.

Barclay Committee (1982) *Social workers: Their roles and tasks* (Barclay Report), London: National Institute for Social Work.

BBC News (2008) 'Boy convicted of £5 bet murder', 22 January (http://news.bbc.co.uk/1/hi/england/wear/7202351.stm).

Becker, H. (1963) *Outsiders: Studies in the sociology of deviance*, New York: Free Press.

Bell, C. and Newby, H. (1971) *Community studies*, London: George Allen & Unwin.

Bellah, R.N., Madsen, R.D., Sullivan, W.M., Swidler, A. and Tipton, S.M. (1985) *Habits of the heart: Individualism and commitment in American life*, Berkeley, CA: University of California Press.

Beresford, P. (nd) *Patch in perspective: Decentralising and democratising social services*, London: Battersea Community Action.

Beresford, P. (2003) *It's our lives: A short theory of knowledge, distance and experience*, London: Citizen Press.

Beresford, P. and Croft, S. (1984) *Patch in perspective: Decentralising and democratising social services*, London: Battersea Community Action.

Berger, P. and Luckman, T. (1966) *The social construction of reality*, Harmondsworth: Penguin Books.

Bisman, C. (1994) *Social work practice: Cases and principles*, Belmont, CA: Wadsworth Publishing Company.

Bradshaw, J. (1972) 'The concept of social need', *New Society*, 30 March.

Buckley, W. (1967) *Sociology and modern systems theory*, Englewood Cliffs, NJ: Prentice Hall.

Burnham, D. (2011) 'Selective memory: a note on social work historiography', *British Journal of Social Work*, vol 41, no 1, pp 5-21.

Carter, H. (2010) 'Police investigate death of man with learning difficulties tormented for years by gangs: 18-year-old held on suspicion of manslaughter as neighbours allege decade of harassment by youths', *The Guardian*, 12 March (www.guardian.co.uk/uk/2010/mar/12/police-investigate-death-man-tormented-gangs).

Clarke, S. (2002) 'The regeneration of communities', in B. Bytheway, V. Bacigalupo, J. Bornat, J. Johnson and S. Spurr (eds) *Understanding care, welfare and community: A reader*, London: Routledge, pp 103-111.

CLG (Department of Communities and Local Government) (2006) *Strong and prosperous communities: The local government White Paper*, London: The Stationery Office.

Cohen, A.P. (1985) *The symbolic construction of community*, New York: Tavistock Publications and Ellis Horwood Limited.

Coote, A. (2010) *Ten big questions about the Big Society: And ten ways to make the best of it*, London: New Economics Foundation.

Couto, R.A. and Guthrie, C.S. (1999) *Making democracy work better: Mediating structures, social capital, and the democratic prospect*, Chapel Hill, NC: University of North Carolina Press.

Cree, V. and Myers, S. (2008) *Social work: Making a difference*, Bristol: The Policy Press.

Day, G. (2006) *Community and everyday life*, New York: Routledge.

Dalley, G. (1988) *Ideologies of caring: Rethinking community and collectivism*, Basingstoke: Macmillan.

Darvill, G. and Smale, G. (eds) (1990) *Partners in empowerment: Networks of innovation in social work*, London: National Institute for Social Work.

Dalrymple, J. and Burke, B. (2006) Anti-oppressive practice: Social care and the law, Maidenhead: Open University Press.

Dean, H. (2010) *Understanding human need*, Bristol: The Policy Press.

Dean, R.G. (1993) 'Constructivism: an approach to clinical practice', *Smith College Studies in Social Work*, vol 63, no 2, pp 127–46.

DH (Department of Health) (1989) *Caring for people: Community care into the next decade and beyond*, London: The Stationery Office.

DH (2000) *Framework for the assessment of children in need and their families: Guidance pack*, London: The Stationery Office.

DH (2002) *Fair Access to Care Services: Guidance on eligibility criteria for adult social care* (LAC (2002)13) (www.dh.gov.uk).

DH (2006) *Our health, our care, our say: A new direction for community services* (www.dh.gov.uk).

DH (2007) *Putting people first: A shared vision and commitment to the transformation of adult social care* (www.dh.gov.uk).

DH (2010) *Guidance on eligibility criteria for adult social care* (www.dh.gov.uk).

DH, DfEE (Department for Education and Employment) and Home Office (2000) *Framework for the assessment of children in need and their families*, London: The Stationery Office.

Dominelli, L. (1993) *Social work: Mirror of society or its conscience?*, Sheffield: Department of Sociological Studies.

Doyal, L. and Gough, I. (1991) *A theory of human need*, Basingstoke: Macmillan.

Earth Charter Initiative, The (2011) *The Earth Charter* (www.earthcharter inaction.org/content/pages/Read-the-Charter.html).

Earth Charter International (2010) *Good practices with the Earth Charter*, San Jose, Costa Rica: UNESCO and Earth Charter International Secretariat.

England, H. (1986) *Social work as art*, London: Allen & Unwin.

Estes, R.J. (1993) 'Toward sustainable development: from theory to praxis', *Social Development Issues*, vol 15, no 3, pp 1–29.

Evans, C. (1997) *From bobble hats to red jackets: A history of the first five years of the Wiltshire and Swindon Users' Network*, Devizes: Wiltshire Community Care Users' Involvement Network.

Falk, R. (1972) *This endangered planet: Prospects and proposal for human survival*, New York: Vintage.

Ferguson, I. (2008) *Reclaiming social work: Challenging neo-liberalism and promoting social justice*, London: Sage Publications.

Ferguson, I. and Woodward, R. (2009) *Radical social work in practice: Making a difference*, Bristol: The Policy Press.

Ferguson, I., Lavalette, M. and Whitmore, E. (eds) (2005) *Globalisation, global justice and social work*, Abingdon: Routledge.

Fook, J. (2002) *Social work: Critical theory and practice*, London: Sage Publications.

Franklin, C. (1995) 'Expanding the vision of the social constructionist debates: creating relevance for practitioners', *Families in Society*, vol 76, no 7, pp 395–406.

Freire, P. (1993) *Pedagogy of the oppressed*, New York: Penguin.

Freire, P. (1996) *Pedagogy of the oppressed* (2nd edn), Harmondsworth: Penguin.

Gamble, D.N. and Hoff, M.D. (2005) 'Sustainable community development', in M. Weil (ed) *The handbook of community practice*, Thousand Oaks, CA: Sage Publications, pp 169–88.

Gamble, D.N. and Weil, M. (2010) *Community practice skills: Local to global perspectives*, New York: Columbia University Press.

Gergen, K.J. (1985) 'The social constructionist movement in modern psychology', *American Psychologist*, vol 40, no 3, pp 266–75.

Germain, C.B. (ed) (1979) *Social work practice: People and environments*, New York: Columbia University Press.

Gilchrist, A. (2004) *The well-connected community: A networking approach to community development*, Bristol: The Policy Press.

Gitterman, A. and Germain, C.B. (2008) *The life model of social work practice: Advances in theory and practice* (3rd edn), New York: Columbia University Press.

Goffman, E. (1963) *Stigma: Notes on the management of spoiled identity*, London: Penguin.

Goldsworthy, J. (2002) 'Resurrecting a model of integrating individual work with community development and social action', *Community Development Journal*, pp 327–37.

Greene, G.J. and Lee, M.Y. (2002) 'The social construction of empowerment', in M. O'Melia and K.K. Miley (eds) *Pathways to power: Readings in contextual social work practice*, Boston, MA: Allyn & Bacon, pp 175–201.

Greene, G.J., Lee, M.Y. and Hoffpauir, S. (2005) 'The language of empowerment and strengths in clinical social work: a constructivist perspective', *Families in Society*, vol 86, no 2, pp 267–77.

Griffiths Report (1988) *Community care: Agenda for action*, London: HMSO.

Hadley, R. and McGrath, M. (1984) *When social services are local: The Normanton experience*, London: Allen & Unwin.

Haire, M., Ghiselli, E.E. and Porter, L.W. (1966) *Managerial thinking: An international study*, New York: Wiley.

Hall, A. and Midgley, J.O. (2004) *Social policy for development*, Thousand Oaks, CA: Sage Publications.

Hanley, B. (2005) *Research as empowerment? Report of a series of seminars organised by the Toronto Group*, York: Joseph Rowntree Foundation.

Hanley, B., Bradbrun, J., Barnes, M., Evans, C., Goodacre, H., Kelson, M., Kent, A., Oliver, S., Thomas, S. and Wallcraft, J. (2004) *Involving the public in NHS public health and social care: Briefing notes for researchers*, Eastleigh: Involve.

Hardcastle, D.A. (2004) 'Globalization, welfare states and social work', in N.-T. Tan and A. Rowlands (eds) *Social work around the world, vol 3*, Berne, Switzerland: International Federation of Social Workers, pp 95-112.

Hardcastle, D.A. (2011) *Community practice: Theories and skills for social workers* (3rd edn), New York: Oxford University Press.

Hargreaves, R. (1982) 'The meaning of community social work', in T. Philpot (ed) *A new direction for social work? The Barclay Report and its implications*, London: IPC Business Press, pp 21-27.

Harris, J. and White, V. (2009) *Modernising social work: Critical considerations*, Bristol: The Policy Press.

Hart, M. (1999) *Guide to sustainable community indicators* (2nd edn), North Andover, MA: Hart Environmental Data.

Hawtin, M. and Percy-Smith, J. (2007) *Community profiling: A practice guide* (2nd edn), Maidenhead: Open University Press.

Hawtin, M., Hughes, G. and Percy-Smith, J. (1994) *Community profiling: Auditing social needs*, Maidenhead: Open University Press.

Heenan, D. (2004) 'Learning lessons from the past or re-visiting old mistakes: social work and community development in Northern Ireland', *British Journal of Social Work*, vol 34, pp 793-809.

Henwood, M. and Hudson, B. (2008) 'Checking the FACS: the government's current system of delivering social care will seriously limit the potential benefits of personalised budgets', *The Guardian*, 13 February.

Hofstede, G. (1980) *Culture's consequences: International differences in work-related values*, London: Sage Publications.

Hofstede, G. (1984) 'The cultural relativity of the quality of life concept', *Academy of Management Review*, vol 9, no 3, pp 389-98.

Hugman, R. (2009) 'But is it social work? Some reflections on mistaken identities', *British Journal of Social Work*, vol 39, pp 1138-53.

Ife, J. (2007) 'The new international agendas: what role for social work?', Hokenstad International Social Work Lecture, Council on Social Work Education, San Francisco, CA.

IFSW (International Federation of Social Workers) (2005) *International policy statement on globalization and the environment* (www.ifsw.org/p38000222.html).

IFSW and IASSW (International Association of Schools of Social Work) (2004) *Ethics in social work, Statement of principles* (www.ifsw.org/f38000032. html).

Jones, C. (2005) 'The neo-liberal assault: voices from the front line of British state social work', in I. Ferguson, M. Lavalette and E. Whitmore (eds) *Globalisation, global justice and social work*, Abingdon: Routledge.

Jordan, B. (2007) *Social work and well-being*, Lyme Regis: Russell House.

Karls, J.M. and Wandrei, K.E. (eds) (1994). *Person-in-environment system: The PIE classification system for social functioning problems*, Washington, DC: NASW Press.

Konopka, G. (1963) *Social group work: A helping process*, Englewood Cliffs, NJ: Prentice-Hall.

Laird, J. (1993) 'Family-centered practice: cultural and constructionist reflections', *Journal of Teaching in Social Work*, vol 8, no 1/2, pp 77–109.

Lawless, P. (2011) 'Big Society and community: lessons from the 1998–2011 New Deal for Communities Programme for England', *People, Place and Policy Online*, vol 5, no 2, pp 55–64.

Lee, J.A.B. (1996) 'The empowerment approach to social work practice', in F.J. Turner (ed) *Social work treatment: Interlocking theoretical approaches* (4th edn), New York: Free Press, pp 218–49.

Le Grand, J. and Bartlett, W. (1993) *Quasi-markets and social policy*, Basingstoke: Macmillan.

Lemert, E. (1972) *Human deviance, social problems and social control* (2nd edn), Englewood Cliffs, NJ: Prentice-Hall.

Leonard, P. (1975) 'Towards a paradigm for radical practice', in R. Bailey and M. Brake (eds) *Radical social work*, London: Edward Arnold.

Loney, M. (1983) *Community against government: The British Community Development Project 1968-1978: A study of government incompetence*, London: Heinemann.

McDonald, A. (2006) *Understanding community care: A guide for social workers*, Basingstoke: Palgrave Macmillan.

McLaughlin, H. (2006) 'Involving young service users as co-researchers: possibilities, benefits and costs', *British Journal of Social Work*, vol 36, pp 1395–410.

Major, J. (1993) Speech to the Conservative Group for Europe, 22 April.

Maslow, A. (1954) *Motivation and personality*, New York: Harper.

Maslow, A. (1970) *Motivation and personality*, New York: Harper & Row.

Matsuoka, J.K. and McGregor, D.P. (1994) 'Endangered culture: Hawaiians, nature and economic development', in M.D. Hoff and J.G. McNutt (eds) *The global environmental crisis: Implications for social welfare and social work*, Aldershot: Avebury Books/Ashgate, pp 100-16.

Mayer, J. and Timms, N. (1970) *The client speaks: Working class impressions of casework*, London: Routledge & Kegan Paul.

Mayo, M. (1994) *Communities and caring: The mixed economy of welfare*, Basingstoke: Macmillan.

Mayo, M. (2009) 'Community work', in R. Adams, L. Dominelli and M. Payne (eds) *Critical practice in social work* (2nd edn), Basingstoke: Palgrave Macmillan, pp 125-136.

Means, R., Richards, S. and Smith, R. (2008) *Community care* (4th edn), Basingstoke: Palgrave Macmillan.

Mendes, P. (2009) 'Teaching community development to social work students: a critical reflection', *Community Development Journal*, vol 44, no 2, pp 248-62.

Midgley, J. (1986) *Community participation, social development and the state*, London: Routledge.

Midgley, J. (1995) *Social development: The developmental perspective in social welfare*, London: Sage Publications.

Midgley, J. and Livermore, M. (2005) 'Development theory and community practice', in M. Weil (ed) *The handbook of community practice*, Thousand Oaks, CA: Sage Publications, pp 153-168.

Mills, C.W. (1959) *The sociological imagination*, Oxford: Oxford University Press.

Motes, P.S. and Hess, P.M. (eds) (2007) *Collaborating with community-based organisations: Through consultation and technical assistance*, New York: Columbia University Press.

NGO (Non-Governmental Organisation) Global Network (2011) *Definition of NGOs* (www.ngo.org/ngoinfo/define.html).

NISW (National Institute for Social Work) (1983) *The Barclay Report: Papers from a consultation day*, NISW Paper No 15, London: NISW.

O'Hagan, S. (2006) 'England my England', *The Observer*, Sunday October 1, 2006.

Ohmer, M. and DeMasi, K. (2009) *Consensus organizing: A community development workbook*, Thousand Oaks, CA: Sage Publications.

Parsloe, P. (1983) 'Community social work: what is it? Is it feasible?', in NISW (National Institute for Social Work), *The Barclay Report: Papers from a consultation day*, NISW Paper No 15, London: NISW, pp 46-53.

Payne, M. (2005) *Modern social work theory* (3rd edn), Basingstoke: Palgrave Macmillan.

Pincus, A. and Minahan, A. (1973) *Social work practice: Model and method*, Itasca, IL: Peacock.

Pincus, A. and Minahan, A. (1977) 'A model for social work practice', in H. Specht and A. Vickery (eds) *Integrating social work methods*, London: George Allen & Unwin, pp 73-104.

Plant, R. (1974) *Community and ideology: An essay in applied social philosophy*, London: Routledge & Kegan Paul.

Powell, M. (1999) *New Labour, new welfare state: The 'third way' in British social policy*, Bristol: The Policy Press.

Putnam, R.D. (2000) *Bowling alone: The collapse and revival of American community*, New York: Simon & Schuster.

Ramesh, R. (2011) 'Charities in fight for survival as finds slashed', *The Guardian*, 2 August.

Reisch, M. (2005) 'Radical community organizing', in M. Weil (ed) *The handbook of community practice*, pp 287-304, Thousand Oaks, CA: Sage.

Roberts-DeGennaro, M. and Mizrahi, T. (2005) 'Coalitions as social change agents', in M. Weil (ed) *The handbook of community practice*, pp 305-18, Thousand Oaks, CA: Sage.

Robson, S. and Spence, J. (2011) 'The erosion of feminist self and identity in community development theory and practice', *Community Development Journal*, vol 46, no 3, pp 288-301.

Saleebey, D. (ed) (2009) *The strengths perspective in social work practice* (5th edn), Boston, MA: Pearson Education.

Saleebey, D. (2001) *Human behavior and social environments: A biopsychosocial approach*, New York: Columbia University Press.

Schon, D. (1984) *The reflective practitioner: How professionals think in action*, New York: Basic Books.

Schwandt, T.A. (2000) 'Three epistemological stances for qualitative inquiry: interpretivism, hermeneutics and social constructionism', in N.K. Denzin and Y.S. Lincoln (eds) *Handbook of qualitative research* (2nd edn), Thousand Oaks, CA: Sage Publications, Inc, pp 189-213.

Seebohm Report (1968) *Report of the Committee on Local Authority and Allied Personal Social Services*, London: HMSO.

Sewpaul, V. (2004) 'Globalization, African governance and the partnership for Africa's development', in N.-T. Tan and A. Rowland (eds) *Social work around the world, vol 3*, Berne, Switzerland: International Federation of Social Workers, pp 30-47.

Sharkey, P. (2007) *The essentials of community care* (2nd edn), Basingstoke: Palgrave Macmillan.

Smale, G. and Bennett, W. (eds) (1989) *Pictures of practice: Volume 1, Community social work in Scotland,* London: National Institute for Social Work, Practice and Development Exchange.

Smale, G., Tuson, G., Biehal, N. and Marsh, P. (1993) *Empowerment, assessment, care management and the skilled worker*, London: The Stationery Office.

Specht, H. and Vickery, A. (eds) (1977) *Integrating social work methods*, London: George Allen & Unwin Ltd.

Stepney, P. and Popple, K. (2008) *Social work and the community: A critical context for practice*, Basingstoke: Palgrave Macmillan.

Teater, B. (2010) *An introduction to applying social work theories and methods*, Maidenhead: Open University Press.

Thatcher, M. (1987) Prime Minister Margaret Thatcher, talking to *Women's Own* magazine, 31 October.

Thomas, J. (1983) *Responses to the Barclay Report: England and Wales, Scotland*, London: National Institute for Social Work.

Thompson, N. (2006) *Anti-discriminatory practice* (4th edn), Basingstoke: Palgrave Macmillan.

Twelvetrees, A. (2008) *Community work*, (4th edn), Basingstoke: Palgrave Macmillan.

Unison (2009) *Not waving but drowning: Paper and pressure in adult social work services* (www.unison.org.uk/acrobat/B4710a.pdf).

UN (United Nations) (2011) *The Millennium Development Goals Report 2011*, New York: UN.

UNDP (United Nations Development Programme) (2000) *Human Development Report 2000*, New York: Oxford University Press.

UNDP (2002) *Annual Report 2002* (www.undp.org/annualreports/2002/english/).

UNDP (2010) *Human Development Report 2010: 20th anniversary edition*, New York: UNDP.

van Wormer, K. and Besthorn, F.H. (2011) *Human behavior and the social environment: Groups, communities, and organizations* (2nd edn), New York: Oxford University Press.

Ward, C. (1973) *Anarchy in action*, London: George Allen & Unwin.

WCED (World Commission on Environment and Development) (1987) *Our common future: From one earth to one world*, New York: Oxford University Press.

Weil, M. (2005) 'Introduction: contexts and challenges for 21st-century communities', in M. Weil (ed) *The handbook of community practice*, Thousand Oaks, CA: Sage Publications, pp 3-33.

Weil, M., Gamble, D.N. and MacGuire, E. (2010) *Community practice skills workbook: Local to global perspectives*, New York: Columbia University Press.

Wells, P. (2011) 'Prospect for a Big Society?', Guest editorial, *Special Issue of People and Place Online*, vol 5, no 2, pp 50-4.

Wilde, O. (1891) *The soul of man under socialism* (www.marxists.org/reference/archive/wilde-oscar/soul-man/index.htm).

Willmott, P. (1989) *Community initiatives, patterns and prospects*, London: Policy Studies Institute.

Witkin, S.L. (1995) 'Family social work: a critical constructionist perspective', *Journal of Family Social Work*, vol 1, no 1, pp 33-45.

World Bank, The (2010) *Defining civil society* (http://go.worldbank.org/4CE7W046K0).

Index